THE LIBRARY
ST. MARY'S COLLEGE OF MARYLAND
ST. MARY'S CITY, MARYLAND 20686

HORACE TALKS

Horace Talks

A TRANSLATION

BY
HENRY HARMON CHAMBERLIN

WITH A PREFACE BY
EDWARD KENNARD RAND

BOOKS FOR LIBRARIES PRESS
FREEPORT, NEW YORK

First Published 1940
Reprinted 1971

INTERNATIONAL STANDARD BOOK NUMBER:
0-8369-6653-8

LIBRARY OF CONGRESS CATALOG CARD NUMBER:
74-179524

PRINTED IN THE UNITED STATES OF AMERICA
BY
NEW WORLD BOOK MANUFACTURING CO., INC.
HALLANDALE, FLORIDA 33009

PREFACE

Horace's *Satires*, or rather *Talks* (*Sermones*), have rarely been allowed to say what they have to say to those who would read them today. Even to students of Latin, the poetry of Horace sometimes does not speak out loud and bold, so delicate is his art and so subtle is the spirit of his comedy. Like all his works his *Satires* must be sipped, not gulped, and sipped again and again, if one would learn their flavor. Horace does not apply to his victims the flail of indignation. He treats them more gently, and more mercilessly, in stripping them of their raiment of pride and prejudice, leaving them in a thin undergarment of folly. Horace's gallery of fools to which he invites us everywhere, is most splendidly displayed in the Third Talk of Book Two. Erasmus, one of Horace's most enlightened pupils, appreciated his master's genial irony, and wrote it large in his memorable *Praise of Folly*.

My friend Chamberlin, too, knows Horace's secret and has revealed it to us in the pages that follow. I have had the privilege of reading and re-reading them as they came fresh from the talented author's pen. He has deftly steered between the Scylla of a word-for-word translation, which means just nothing, and the Charybdis of a rendering into flippant slang. The flavor is ancient. It is Horace who speaks, and yet he speaks as one of us.

Moreover, the author has happily chosen the stateliest

of the metres of English verse, the heroic couplet. For is not Horace's dactylic hexameter the heroic measure of antiquity? This he chose with unerring taste from the various metres displayed by his master Lucilius. Horace does not reproduce the majestic hexameter of Lucretius or that with which his friend Virgil in his novel *Eclogues* had captivated Rome. Horace, essentially a lyric poet of high seriousness, had already exhibited that kind of verse in some of his *Epodes*, notably the Sixteenth. He now turns aside for a *jeu d'esprit*, true to his principle of "speaking truth with a smile." For this he instinctively perfects a new form, a conversational hexameter, no less an achievement in art than his many experiments in lyric. Lucilius gave him the model, in verses vigorous and rude and wordy — the raw material for the sculptor's chisel. The metre has another advantage; by its very nature, it lends itself to Horace's bent for mock-heroic and parody, no less than to his serious reflections and to his counsels for life. And all the while, whatever the flights, up or down or roundabout, the poet's words are those of conversation.

So all the elements of Horace's art, both in its spirit and in its form, come to life again in Chamberlin's translation. Gentle reader, *lege feliciter*.

EDWARD KENNARD RAND

Cambridge, Massachusetts
July, 1940

CONTENTS

PREFACE 5
INTRODUCTION 9

Book I

I LUST OF MONEY 21
II WOMEN AND THE GOLDEN MEAN 31
III ON BEING HUMANE 41
IV HOW TO WRITE SATIRE 51
V THE JOURNEY 61
VI HORACE AND HIS FATHER 69
VII THE PUN 79
VIII PRIAPUS AND WITCHES 83
IX THE PEST 89
X POETIC CLIQUES 95

Book II

I A LAWYER'S OPINION 105
II PLAIN LIVING 111
III STOIC HARANGUE 121
IV DE RERUM NATURA 143
V HOW TO GET RICH QUICK 149
VI " OF THE MEAN AND SURE ESTATE " . . . 157
VII MASTER AND SLAVE 165
VIII THE BANQUET 175

INTRODUCTION

WHY TRANSLATE the satires of Horace? He has already been translated for nearly fifteen centuries. His maxims have so permeated and pervaded the English language that a large number of contemporary scribblers are actually writing Horace, when they think they are expressing their own ideas. Why add to a thousand versions, and seek to familiarize a subject already familiar?

The answer is that today the influence of Horace is more real than apparent. A great many people consider his poems as museum pieces of an interest wholly antiquarian. They do not realize that Horace, like the Parthenon, is perennially up-to-date; that what he has to say is usually as vital to the present as it was to the Augustan age. He is like a dear old friend who will sit down with you in your study and converse with you about matters where ignorance is bad, *nescire malum est* — a friend whose subtle and infectious humor, sometimes tinged with the sadness which finds a fuller expression in his *Odes*, will impart to you the quintessence of the worldly wisdom of the ancients.

> "*Horace still charms with graceful negligence*
> *And, without method, talks you into sense;*
> *Will, like a friend, familiarly convey*
> *The truest notions in the easiest way.*"

Pope is right, then and now. And this is the main reason for a fresh interpretation of Horace, especially since modern research has told us a great deal about him which was unknown to Pope and Boileau. Such interpretation may counteract such hatred of Horace as the pedagogues implanted in the youthful bosoms of Byron and Tennyson, and make him loved as he deserves to be loved.

Horace has written his autobiography. The story of his life is told in his verses, though not as a connected narrative. He was born on the eighth of December, in the year 65 B.C. His father, probably a public slave of the township of Venusia, earned enough money to purchase his own freedom and give his son the best education the times afforded. Horace went to Rome, and was finishing at Athens when Julius Caesar was struck down in the Roman Senate. He fought on the side of Brutus at Philippi, where he " threw away his shield " in the fashion of three Greek poets before him, and he afterwards got back to Rome under a general amnesty. There he began life anew as a clerk in the Quaestor's office; but in a few years his poems and his personality had won him the patronage of Maecenas and the friendship of the noblest Romans of them all. And he has been making friends ever since.

" *Non omnis moriar*," he wrote in the last Ode of the third book — " I shall not wholly die "; and, as he says immediately afterwards, a great part of him has escaped from the goddess of Death. He has gone down the ages and made friends throughout western civilization, and his two thousandth birthday was celebrated all over Europe and America. Who can number the generations that have responded to his appeal? Ever since the days of Augustus and Maecenas his influential friends have abounded. At the court of Charlemagne, the good abbot Alcuin, that ecclesiastical and literary luminary from Yorkshire, assumed the name of Flaccus when he was among his cronies. Dante had what might be called a bowing acquaintance with *Orazio Satirico* and enrolled him among the world's five great poets, although the Horatian sense of humor could hardly have appealed to the grim, intense, and rhapsodic genius of the great Florentine. The Middle Ages passed and gave way to the Renaissance, but Horace remained. Spenser paid homage to his precepts and Milton to his example. Ben Jonson, Herrick, Donne, Cowley, and Dryden joined the chorus. He was given *les grandes entrées* to the literary circles at the court of Louis XIV; and throughout the Eighteenth Century, both in France and England, *De Arte Poetica* was a standard for the rules of poetic composition, and he was acclaimed as the " guide, philosopher, and friend " of all the versemakers. Matthew Prior began his career by explaining a passage from the *Odes* to the Earl of Dorset. Addison can almost be described as a little Horace. Novelists imitated him, and statesmen quoted him in Parliament. And in later years, men of such diverse talents as Samuel Johnson, Edmund Burke, William Pitt, and William Cowper were among his devotees.

Of the many editions published at this period, the most famous is that of Bentley, where the text is emended rather more brilliantly than judiciously. But Pine's *Horace* is the choicest of them all. The first volume, the *Odes and Epodes,* came out in 1733; and the second, containing the *Satires and Epistles*, followed four years later. The text, the vignettes, and the list of subscribers, are all engraved on copper plate, and the result is an exquisite curio. Even the list of subscribers makes interesting reading. Among these friends of Horace were Frederick, Prince of Wales, and his brother, the Duke of Cumberland, who fourteen years later was to break the power of Prince Charley. There were the Kings of England, France, Spain, and Portugal, and the Old Pretender; also Prince Frederick of Hesse Cassel, under which title masqueraded Frederick the Great, then Crown Prince of Prussia, because his father, like some of our moderns, was "agin the classics." There were Sir Robert Walpole, Prime Minister of England, and the Duke of Berwick, who shared the exile of the House of Stuart; across the Atlantic there were the Right Honorable, the Lord Baltimore, and His Excellency Jonathan Belcher, "Esqre, Captain, General, and Governor in Chief of His Majesty's Province of ye Massachusetts Bay and New Hampshire."

With others of less note came the purely literary men, — the Reverend Dr. Jonathan Swift, Dean of St. Patrick, who received a copy of the first volume, elegantly bound, for a birthday present; also Alexander Pope, who had brought out the *Dunciad;* and Colley Cibber, who was later to be figured — or disfigured — as its hero. And I might mention Bubb Doddington and William Hogarth, etcher of manners and morals, who later caricatured the portly John Pine as the friar in his "Gate of Calais." What visions that list conjures up! The Grotto at Twickenham "composed of marbles, spars, gems, ores and minerals"; the laurels in the garden of the Dublin Deanery, from "whose upper chambers well lined with antique books and books new coined," there issued forth *Gulliver's Travels* and the *Drapier's Letters* and many other examples of the *saeva indignatio* of the illustrious author; the courtyard of Windsor Castle, well lined with gilt coaches whose bewigged, bepatched and bepowdered occupants, with their stars and garters and knee breeches and hoop skirts, were dancing attendance at the Queen's drawing room; and the field of Culloden, where the stone cairns of the Highland clans gleamed silent in the moonlight; and the spirit of Horace brooding over them all. *Beatus ille qui procul negotiis; post equitem sedet atra cura; dulce et decorum est pro patria mori.*

The old regime went out and the romantic movement came in, but the influence of Horace persisted, not paramount as in the days of Pope and Dryden, but still a powerful persuader. It is true that Walter Savage Landor declaimed against him; that Lowell and Arnold belittled his genius; and that Thomas Carlyle in a frenzy of romantic revolt that was intensified by dyspepsia, asserted emphatically that he had no use for the Golden Mean. But Horace still had his champions — Gladstone among the statesmen, Thackeray among the novelists, Austin Dobson among the critics; and among the poets, Shelley and Wordsworth and Browning and Tennyson, who had got over his early dislike when as a man he put away childish things. At the close of the century Horace could number Robert Louis Stevenson among his friends, and also Rudyard Kipling, whose virile genius pays, in his *Regulus*, a magnificent tribute to the patriotism and moral stamina of the Augustan poet. In our turgid days of a mental and moral aberration and upheaval that threatens to engulf all saner traditions, Horace still keeps on making friends; and the more he makes, the better for us all.

Such is the influence and personality which I have tried

to reproduce in a translation of the *Satires*. The *Odes* I should never attempt. There have been a great many versions, and every one I have come across seems to me painfully inadequate. For the form and substance are so interfused that when you alter the one, you destroy the other. But the *Satires* are another story. They are largely in colloquial Latin, which can be rendered roughly into colloquial English. But there are other qualities of style which Horace himself outlines in the tenth satire of the first book. Frequently he adopts the mock heroic, in a somewhat irreverent imitation of Homer and the Greek tragedians. Frequently there are poetic bits of description or of characterization that shine through the conversational verse which Horace likens to prose. The style varies often from line to line, and sometimes even in a single sentence. The humor is heightened by what Horace seems to consider high-flown phraseology, which ends in an abrupt turn to the ludicrous; for Horace is a past master of anticlimax. Yet often his high-flown images are so exquisitely wrought that they have an imperishable lyric beauty of their own. Horace is a very self-conscious artist, but he cannot help being poetic even when he is being funny.

Let us turn from his style to his delineation of character. Besides his many passages of self-portrayal, Horace gives us examples to enforce his maxims, and each example is a concrete individual. With incredible brevity he can put before us various characters who stand out so vividly from his verse that we think of them as living persons. In his description of his father, we actually meet the fine old fellow himself, with his homely horse sense and his indefatigable determination to make a man out of his son. Ofellus, the staunch old farmer who will not allow himself to be downcast by the dispossession of his farm, has endeared himself to many readers. But there are also much sillier characters whom Horace shows up in a ridiculous light, though often with a kindly tolerance for their folly — Davus, the impertinent slave; Damasippus, the garrulous business man who loses his money, tries to sell antiques, and finally becomes a Stoic philosopher; Nasidienus, the parvenu who poses as an epicure and gives a great banquet in honor of Maecenas, which through his foolish self-conceit turns out to be a failure; Persius the Levantine millionaire, and his adversary Rupilius King, the renegade Italian; the naive rustic mouse and his highfalutin city friend — you can go on with the enumeration but you will not find a single or married woman who is sympathetically portrayed by Horace. In the *Odes* he pays some charming compliments to pretty young girls, and also high tribute to the indomitable valor of a beautiful and unfortunate queen. But in the *Satires* he shows himself a man's man and a man's poet, and a faithful friend to a few select souls. He admired the sturdy virtues of the countryside as much as he detested the city-bred degeneracy of the Roman mob. He is a keen and profound observer of mankind, with the emphasis on the man.

Such is the poet whose *Satires* I have tried to translate. I have tried, in so far as in me lies, to get inside of Horace's skin, as he himself might say; to ascertain what effect he had on his contemporaries and to reproduce it for modern readers. I am aware that this method is anathema to a number of more or less erudite persons, including Matthew Arnold among the more erudite. They assert that we know practically nothing of what the ancient Romans felt on most subjects, and can therefore form no idea of the impression Horace made. But I think that these arbiters of the classics rather overstate their case. After all, we do know something of the inhabitants of Rome in the days of Augustus. We know, for example, that normally they had two eyes, two ears, a Roman nose, and a mouth; that they laughed when they were tickled and objected when they were hurt; that some of them liked good things to eat and drink; that some of them approved of martial exercise; that many were fond of looking on at sports and games of a rough nature; that some were money-grabbers; that others were dissipated; that certain individuals cultivated philosophy and the Muses, both Greek and Latin; and that the leaders were more intelligent than the electorate. Moreover, recent archeological research has unearthed many memorials which throw a light on the material side of their civilization. We have enough to form an estimate, even if imperfect, of how they might be impressed by satire. It seems to me that we might as well make the most of what we know, instead of throwing up the sponge because we are not omniscient.

Audaciously, perhaps, I have tried to catch the spirit of the original. I have taken as my medium the heroic couplet, because as a norm it is analogous in English to the hexameter in Greek and Latin. I have expanded as little as I could, except for a definite effect, or for the explanation of a reference which would otherwise require a footnote. I have tried to copy the tone-color of the lines, Horace being a master of what is rather horrendously called the art of onomatopoeia, of making the sound "seem an echo of the sense." I have tried to adopt the "big bowwow" when Horace adopts it, and to talk casually when he chats. I have tried, however ineptly, to reproduce the flashes of poetic splendor which so often illuminate his verse. I realize how hard it is to put oneself in the place of an ancient poet. But however far an individual may fall short, I do not believe that such an aim is inherently impossible.

Finally I would register my conviction that poetry is the only medium for translating poetry. I have read a number of prose versions of Horace. They do very well as trots, but they give no adequate idea of the original. They are more or less verbally correct, but they no more resemble the wise and whimsical friend of Maecenas and Virgil than the man in the moon. I cannot imagine how anybody who perused them would want to have anything more to do with Horace. They are poor pallid productions, featureless and as dry as dust. I fancy that Horace, with his horror of being used as a textbook, would write about them with less than his accustomed urbanity. I am presumptuous enough to hope that he would treat such efforts as mine with a little more indulgence; that his smile would be a kindly smile, and his ridicule, a kindly ridicule.

HORACE TALKS

BOOK I

BOOK I

I · LUST OF MONEY

THE FIRST talk was probably composed sometime between 38 and 33 B.C., after Horace was numbered among the friends of Maecenas and before he was given the Sabine farm. The apostrophe to Maecenas may have been written last of all.

None of the ideas originated with Horace, as he himself implies in his gibe at Crispinus at the finale. Examples of the violation of the Golden Mean were the stock in trade of Greek Philosophy. They had been imported many years before from Athens and Alexandria and had been preached about and written about by Cicero and Lucilius and countless others. But some of them were here crystallized by Horace's genius and have come down to us as bright as when they were first fashioned for the *Sermo*.

The studied discursiveness of style, which may be regarded as the precursor of the essay, has been copied in France by such writers as Regnier and Boileau, and in England by a procession of poets from Sir Thomas Wyatt to William Cowper. Perhaps the most notable English exponents were Dryden and Pope, though neither of them attained the urbane spirit of Horatian humor; for Dryden was too imperious and Pope too spiteful.

The truisms which Horace has crystallized are true for us today; and I am afraid they will continue to be true. Contemporary examples put their funds into safe deposit boxes instead of a hole in the ground, and worry less about burglars than the fluctuations of the stock market. But has the worship of the Almighty Dollar wholly departed from our shores? If not, these old saws can be taken to heart by modern instances.

The ant comes from Aesop. But the fabulist seems to think of her as an individual whose hibernation is akin to that of the squirrel. Apparently he does not know that most ants go to sleep in the winter and do not need to eat. Moreover, he seems to ignore the activities of the ant hill — which might be called a formic Soviet, where all intelligence is strictly on a communistic level, and even black ants are red!

The irate Jupiter with puffed out cheeks, comes off the comic stage. So far as I know, we have had no such travesty of the Supreme Being in Christendom until the advent of *Green Pastures*.

Cowley is the only direct translator of this talk whom I have come across. He has made a fluent paraphrase of the first half in his essay on Avarice.

Talk One

How come, Maecenas, none contentedly
Mind their own business, whether it may be
Given by choice or chance to come their ways?
The other fellow's job gets all the praise,
" These merchants are in luck," the soldier swears,   5
With shattered limbs from hard laborious years.
The merchant is contrarious in mind,
His vessel tossed about by southern wind:
" I'd rather be a soldier; yes indeed;
The hour is come to charge. The moments lead   10
To sudden death or joyous victory."
The farmer is extolled by such as be
Trained in the law's procedure, even more
At cockcrow, when the client storms the door.
The country man, enjoined to come to town,   15
To certify his bond with money down,
Exclaims that only those are really well
Off, who inside the city limits dwell.
And many another I might mention thus,
Enough to bore loquacious Fabius.   20
To cut it short, no longer to delay,
Listen, here is the point. Some god might say:
" Well, here I am; and what you like to be
I'll make you. What you want, you'll get from me.
Old soldier, you can be a merchant now;   25

And jurisconsult, you can drive the plow;
Get going: Each one take the other's part.
Hey! hey! Still sticking round? " They will not start
To do the very thing they said they had at heart.
Jupiter's right, when he puffs out both cheeks,   30
And in his indignation, thus he speaks:
" Never again shall I so easy be.
To lend my ear to such a votary."
Moreover I will not the time beguile
With wisecracks, though they often are worthwhile.   35
What is the harm to tell truth with a smile?
As teachers with ingratiating ease
Give biscuits to the boys for A. B. C.'s.
Nevertheless, we'll put aside our play
And take the question in a serious way.   40
The man who turns hard ground with plow as hard,
Mine host, who cheats you out of his reward,
The soldier, and the sailors who must be
Reckless enough to run through every sea,
Say they will stand for work, with this in mind;   45
When they grow old, they safely leave behind
Their toil for rations in an ample hoard.
The little ant example may afford,
Who with great labor carries in her jaws
Whatever she can get of hips and haws,   50
And shrewd and provident for what may come,
Adds to her pile and swells her store at home.
But when upon the turning of the year,
With sad Aquarius the heavens are blear,
No more she will creep out, for she is wise;   55
And what she sought, she then may utilize.
But you from gain no scorching summer day

Can stop. Fire, sea, nor sword will block your way,
While some one else more coin has in hold.
What use, a mighty weight of silver and gold 60
If furtively afraid to be so rich,
You put it on deposit in a ditch?
" But when you break it up, your pile is spent,
And what is left will not be worth a cent."
Even if you don't, why is your pile so fine? 65
Your stomach cannot hold more food than mine
Although your threshing floor treads out in wheat
A hundred thousand barrels fit to eat.
If in a slave gang, you went out for sale,
And laden was your shoulder with a bale 70
Of bread, you'll get no more upon the road
Than one who carried nothing of your load.
Really it is no different for a man
Who lives within the bound of Nature's plan
Whether he plows a hundred acres, or 75
A thousand. " But a comfortable store
Is sweet to draw from." Now if, by your leave,
From our small pantries we are to receive
An equal share, what is there more to prize
In yours, that comes from bursting granaries? 80
If you need water only for a jug
To fill, or just enough to fill a mug,
Why say: " I much prefer my drop to bring
From a great river rather than a spring? "
So will it come to all who take delight 85
In more abundance than is just and right.
Fierce Aufidus tears off his banks and they
And these together, all are swept away.
But any man who moderation heeds,

And only craves the little that he needs, 90
Will never draw up water mixed with mud,
Nor send his life away upon the flood.

But mostly men, deceived by false desire,
Remark, " It's not enough which you require.
You're just as much as what you have," they say. 95
What can you do with folks that talk that way?
Tell them where they get off, and let them be
Unhappy. Let them hug their misery.
Like an Athenian, so the story goes,
Lousy with money, who turned up his nose 100
At public disapproval. " People hiss
Me. I myself applaud myself for this,
When I my safety box have opened wide
To contemplate my money that's inside."
Tantalus tried to capture in his drouth 105
A river always flying from his mouth.
Why laugh? Change round the name and when you're
  through
You'll find the story can be told on you.
At money bags you've piled up everywhere,
You gape; you go to sleep on them right there; 110
So sacred are they, that you now command
Yourself to lay on them no impious hand;
On them you still must fix your gloating gaze
As one whom picture paintings might amaze.
Why, don't you know what money's all about, 115
And what's the use of it, to put it out?
It buys you bread and cabbages and wine
And other things without which humans pine
If they can't get them. But by day and night

Scared in your soul, to tremble with affright   120
At big bad thieves or fire or slaves that they
Will loot your hoard before they run away,
Is that so nice and helpful? As for me,
From goods like these, I more than poor would be.
" But if your body's racked with sudden chills   125
Or you are fixed in bed with other ills,
You'll have a nurse the poultice to prepare
And call the doctor in to cure you there,
So he can give you with his medications
Back to your children and your dear relations? "   130
Not much! your wife won't want you to get well;
Your son will say that you can go to hell;
For all your neighbors, everyone you know,
Even the boys and girls, they hate you so.
No wonder they grow hot under the collar,   135
Above them all you put the silver dollar.
Who of them all would offer so to serve
You with affection which you don't deserve?
Or if a kinsman, Nature freely gave,
Or kindly Friendship, you would keep and save,   140
Poor fool, whose money is your guiding star,
Why lose your labor being what you are,
As if a jackass anybody trains
To run along a racetrack with the reins?
So then, there ought to be a limit set   145
To money-chasing. For the more you get
The less you'll be afraid of going in
The red. Enjoy your profit and begin
To wind up your affairs. Don't make a fuss
Over them, like the man Ummidius.   150
The story won't be long. The fellow had

Barrels of money; but his clothes were bad.
He dressed as dirtily as any slave;
And always worried, even to his grave,
That overcome at last with penury   155
He would be sunk. A girl he had made free
Was brave as Clytemnestra through and through;
She with her hatchet split him right in two.
"Well, what's your argument? Like Naerius
To lead my life, or like Nomentanus?"   160
How you run on! You pit each opposite
Against the other in a headlong fight.
Because I tell you not to spare each crumb,
You need not be a washout or a bum.
'Twixt Tanais and Visellius' father-in-law 165
There is a medium from whence to draw
Reason — determined bounds on either hand —
Inside or out the right can never stand.
And so from where I wandered, I return.
There is no tightwad who can ever learn   170
Self-approbation; who would rather not
Prefer the job the other fellow's got;
All folded up with envy, the poor shoat,
Because another fellow has a goat
With bigger udder than his own will bear. 175
So with the poor men's crowd, he'll not compare
Himself; but this or that one he will see
Who seems a little better off than he
And try to distance these and win the cup;
Always the richer man will speed him up.   180
As when the hoofbeats, galloping apace,
Speed up the chariot's starting in the race,
Close pressing those in front the charioteer

Don't give a damn for who brings up the rear.
But rarely we shall find a man who says 185
That he has lived contented with his days,
Retiring from his life, a well-fed guest
Who after dinner hies him to his rest.
But now's enough. You'd think I undertook
To plagiarize Crispinus' cockeyed book, 190
The stoic doggerel of a blinking bore.
And after that, I'll add not one word more.

BOOK I

II · Women and the Golden Mean

Victorian editors and translators have fought shy of Talk Two, where Horace calls a spade a spade with a vengeance. But we cannot get a full length portrait of him without it. It was probably written shortly after he got back to Rome, when the cause of the Republic was lost. It is pungent with the bravado of a restive and impecunious young man, of an outsider who is taking his fling at the scandals of high society. A patrician whom Horace lampooned, became afterwards one of his best friends, when he had risen to the position to which his talents entitled him. In none of his subsequent work is his invective quite so uncompromising.

Pope translated Talk Two very freely, and then disavowed the translation. The bard of Twickenham called it a "Sermon against Adultery," which it is not. Horace is preaching against excess in sexual indulgence, just as in the first *Sermo* he advocates moderation in money making. Adultery was but one of a number of horrible examples, especially horrible because it was so severely punished by Roman Law. The Galba whom he mentions was probably not a guilty party, but a forward-looking citizen who tried to mitigate the pains and penalties. I imagine Horace made fun of the judge, not with any *arrière pensée*, but because he himself was innately conservative.

This is the one talk which does not square with modern conventions. Much that may seem cynical and brutal to us would have appeared less crude to the Augustans. The idea of a censor of public morals, like Cato the Elder, recommending licensed dives in language that today might be used privately by a corrupt party boss, may seem preposterous. But such were the manners and customs of the ancients. Solon felt the same way, according to Philemon as quoted by Athenaeus. Moreover, the remarks of the new Comedian and those of Euboulus about the inmates of such institutions would indicate Hellenic sources. But I will not dwell further on a subject that is not often discussed nowadays in public. Those who can tolerate opinions they do not agree with, may get a laugh out of the *Sermo*. Aunt Mattie and Uncle Squaretoes had better not read it. They will find plenty besides for amusement and edification.

Talk Two

The gypsy women's league that none can rape,
Clown, fakir, beggar and showgirl hang out crape.
Tigellius, their bard, is underground;
For all that crowd he threw the money round.
By contrast, here's a man who, above all   5
Afraid he may be called a prodigal,
From any needy friend would help withhold
To keep away stark hunger or the cold.
But if you ask another fellow why
Down red lane he makes the money fly,   10
His proud ancestral fortune all run through
With loans for fol-de-rols on his menu,
He answers, he'll not be considered blinded
By avarice; he'll not be narrow-minded.
For this may some commend him; others blame.   15
Fufidius, afraid to get the name
Of waster, rich in land, and even more
In principal that hefty interest bore,
Five times the regular profit he would shave
From any sum he for a loan outgave,   20
Preliminary discount from the fund.
The more you lost, the harder you got dunned.
Even a boy who just had come of age
To wear the manly toga, he would page

If pater were supposedly severe. 25
Who would not say, " Good God! " such things to hear?
" From such a profit, much can be expended."
You'd hardly think how little he befriended
Himself. Once Terence put upon the stage
An old man's expiation for curst rage 30
Against a son cast out and gone to sea;
That father used himself no worse than he.
Now if you ask me what it's all about,
It's this way. From a vice some fools get out,
Then to the opposite make haste to go. 35
Maltinus ambles, tunic trailing low;
Another gentleman, fine as fine can be
So highly tucked, his talliwag you see.
Rufillus chews up scent; and all may note
His smell; Gargonius is like a goat. 40
There is no happy medium. Some will not
Touch any woman, if she has not got
A gown whose flounces cover up her heels.
Another for a girl no passion feels
Who will not in a stinking brothel stand. 45
For an acquaintance coming out: " How grand! "
Was Cato's venerable opinion.
" Young man, what you have done, was nobly done!
When with base lust, the arrant vein must swell,
Go to a fancy house, and you'll do well. 50
You'll find the girls all ready for your use,
And other people's wives you'll not seduce."
For Cupiennius that would never go.
" I'll say I'll not be recommended so."
He likes a quoniam dolled up in white. 55
Only a lady gives him true delight.

Women and the Golden Mean

It's worth your while, if you don't like to see
Mankind successful in adultery,
To listen how their labors come to grief,
What risk they run for pleasures rare and brief,   60
Wholly corrupted by most cruel woes.
One man jumps off a roof and down he goes;
And one is whipped to death; and one in flight
Falls among thieves, who do not treat him right;
One paying cash to keep himself intact;   65
One pizzled on by scullions for his act;
Occasionally, with iron it befalls
That someone gleans a lively tail and balls.
All vote that such is lawful punishment,
Only Judge Galba ruling in dissent.   70

But there's another class and safer too
For all who would that kind of business do,
These lovely ladies of a low degree;
With such Sallustius made more than free,
Crazy as one who would commit adultery.   75
If only modest bargains he had made
Within his means as Reason would persuade
Prudently liberal he could pay his pet
As much as any girl would want to get,
More than enough for him to save his face   80
And not involve his ruin and disgrace.
Oh! no! He hugged himself for this alone
With amative and laudatory tone:
"I never took another fellow's wife;
I never touched a matron in my life."   85
Marsaeus, taken with Origo's charm,
Gave to the showgirl country house and farm.

"Other men's wives will never do for me,"
He said. It may be true, in company
With showgirls and paid women of ill fame   90
You need not lose much more than your good name.
Is it enough a lecher's role to shun
And not the actual deed that he has done?
A damaged reputation's not so good
Nor rich inheritance stuck in the mud.   95
What then would be the difference any more
In sinning with a matron or a whore?
Villius was taken in by Fausta's name
And thus betrayed to very open shame.
The people called him Sulla's son-in-law.   100
For him, alas, alack, the deal was raw;
He paid the piper more than was enough;
With fist and iron he first was treated rough
And then kicked out of doors, while high and wide
And handsome, Longarenus rode inside.   105
Well might John Thomas to his owner say,
Seeing how much hard luck had come their way,
"What's biting you? I don't require a quiff
With consular connections, when I'm stiff.
I don't think much of any robe of rank.   110
For all you've got, you have yourself to thank."
What could he say? " A daughter I prefer
With popper in the social register."
Teeming with all the wealth that in her lies,
Oh, how much better Nature could advise   115
Foresquare against your words in open fight
If only you will guide yourself aright,
And do not mess up everything you ought
To shun, with everything that should be sought.

Is there no difference if your troubles rise 120
From force of circumstance or from your vice?
Don't chase the matrons or you will be sorry;
The only fruits you pluck are toil and worry.

With emeralds green and snowy pearls encased,
A matron may be to Cerinthus' taste; 125
But is for this her thigh more delicate,
And is her leg more shapely and more straight?
Why very frequently you'll find a frail
Who'll show you better goods put up for sale.
Moreover all she has, without disguise 130
You'll see, her charms laid bare before your eyes,
Right in the showcase, very fair and plain.
For hidden blemishes, you'll look in vain.
It is the custom of the rich and great,
When trading for a horse in royal state, 135
To look it over covered, so that they
At first inspection shall not go astray;
So from a handsome shape they'll hold aloof
If propped up from below with a soft hoof;
So gaping buyers need not be misled 140
With a fine haunch, arched neck or little head.
All well and good. But do not try to trace
With Lynceus' eyes a lovely form and face
While blinder than Hypsaea you shall be
To all the faults that anyone may see. 145
" What arms and legs! " you cry. But bear in mind
The huge proboscis and the lank behind;
And don't ignore what patently is wrong,
The waist that's all too short, the foot too long.
A matron shows you nothing but her face, 150

The rest, unless she stand in Catia's place,
Her clothes are hiding, whether good or bad;
And you see nothing, though it drives you mad.
As with a rampart compassed round about,
A thousand, thousand things will shut you out, 155
Pages, beauticians, maids, her palanquin
And female hangers-on of humble mien;
The dress that falls straight to the ankles down;
The long mantilla wrapped about the gown;
While everything conspires to hinder you, 160
And so prevent an unimpeded view.
As for the other, in her Coan dress,
You hardly see much more than nakedness.
Club foot nor crooked leg can hidden lie.
You measure out her figure with your eye. 165
Why had you rather by a cheat get done
Before you see the value of your mon?
" The hunter when the skies are overcast
And snow lies deep, will brave the wintry blast
To trail the game and track it to its lair. 170
But never will he touch a sitting hare."
So sings the poet; so his measures move
To application: " Thus it is with Love.
All in his grasp he lightly passes by,
In hot pursuit of what will farthest fly." 175
With these small verses, would you hope in vain
To drive away the passion and the pain,
The raging heat that will not let you rest,
And all the cares that weigh down on your breast?
Ah! would it not be better to inquire 180
What Nature sets for medium of desire,
What possible fulfilment can be tried,

Women and the Golden Mean

And what must be, though painfully denied?
Sever the solid good from empty show.
When thirst burns up your jaws, who then would
    go   185
After a cup of gold? With hunger's need
Gripped, would you only on a peacock feed
Or turbot? Would you then fastidious turn
From all the other food you might discern?
Or when your passion swells, would you pass by   190
A pretty slave who gives you the glad eye?
Wouldn't you rather your attentions thrust
On her, than leave your dynamo to bust?
I would. With giddy girls when I'd be mating,
I'd like them easy and accommodating.   195
The kind who say "A little later on,"
" I want more money," " When my husband's gone,"
In Philodemus' words, are only meant
For Gallic priests who must be continent.
The girl I choose, must never come too dear   200
Nor show up late, when I would have her near;
Fair-haired and straight and comely to be seen;
And I would have her tolerably clean.
Bleached blondes who wear high heels, I do not crave.
Let her put on alone what Nature gave.   205
So side by side, squeezing each other tight,
She on the left and I upon the right,
For me she may indeed be Ilia
Or I will call her my Egeria
Or any other name she may prefer.   210
I'll never be afraid along with her
Of hubby from the country who may hark
Back. Gates are battered down; the dog will bark;

In all the house that fracas will resound,
While on the chamber door, his fist will pound. 215
Pale as a ghost, the wife leaps out of bed.
Loud shrieks the maid, she wishes she was dead!
She fears a broken leg; the wife for pelf
Her dowry brought; and I for just myself.
I run away half dressed, without my shoes; 220
For otherwise my money I shall lose
Or ruin my behind and my good name.
And capture is a miserable shame.
That plea, if made in court, you cannot beat,
Even with Fabius on the judgment seat. 225

BOOK I

III · ON BEING HUMANE

THE Darwinian schedule of human progress is adapted from Lucretius. Otherwise Horace speaks for himself and so does the *Sermo*.

The bewhiskered Stoic philosopher whose regal equilibrium is upset by naughty little boys, is sharply etched. It is remarkable how vividly Horace can portray a personality with such paucity of detail. You are given just enough to fill in the picture for yourself. The funny old man with his extravagant doctrines and his overweening self-importance is used at the end of this talk, just as Tigellius is used at the beginning, as an example of the violation of the Golden Mean.

There is one passage where Horace tells us how a father will euphemize a son's physical defects. The epithets are cognomens of famous Roman families. I have tried to approach the spirit of the original by substituting well-known Americans. If the matter ever comes to their notice, I hope these gentlemen will excuse me for taking liberties with their surnames.

Talk Three

All singers have this fault. When they're among
Friends, if they are requested for a song,
Nothing can induce them. But they'll sing
When nobody has asked for anything,
And not leave off, if only in the mood.   5
Sardinian Tigellius was a good
Example. If Caesar, able to compel,
Begged for his father's sake, his own as well,
Even Augustus could not do a thing.
But if in form, Tigellius would sing;   10
From antipasto to dessert, he'd cry
" O Bacchus! " while his voice would rise on high
Or sink to lowest note of four-stringed lyre.
That man was never steadfast in desire.
Often he ran as flying from a foe;   15
And very often he would walk as slow
As some one carrying Juno's sacred vase.
He often had two hundred slaves to grace
His promenade; and often only ten.
Sometimes he would talk big, like kings of men,   20
Or tetrarchs. At another time he'd say:
" If only a three-legged table came my way
With fine white salt inside a cockle shell,
And mantle coarse but warm, I'd do quite well."
But if this frugal paragon, you hand   25

A wad of money, up to fifty grand,
In five days' time, you'd find, if you should look,
Nothing whatever in his pocketbook.
He'd stay awake all night, until the gray
Of dawn, and then proceed to snore all day.   30
There never was a man so thoroughly
Unequal. Some one now might say to me:
" Have you no faults or failures to confess? "
" Oh yes! but different, and maybe less."
Maenius was censoriously severe   35
On absent Novius. Some one said: " See here!
Are you so ignorant, you think that goes
With us? For all that talk, do you suppose
We don't know you? What are you giving us? "
" Myself I will ignore," said Maenius.   40
Such love of self is impiously stupid;
And more than blameworthy, that kind of Cupid.
When with sore eyes, gummed up with mercury,
The evil you have done you scarcely see,
Why of friends' failings, such sharp notice take   45
As eagle, or the Epidaurian snake?
That sort of thing will all come home to you,
When people ask what's wrong with what you do.
A man's irascible, and therefore less
Prone to endure nosey censoriousness;   50
While on the other hand, you laugh at one
Who needs a shave, whose toga is undone,
Whose wornout shoes flap all around his feet;
And yet for solid worth, you cannot beat
Him. There's no better man. Your friend besides;   55
In that ungainly shape, great genius hides.
Go, shake yourself; and then perhaps you'll see

If natural faults in you implanted be,
Or else bad habits. You may find, in turn,
In your neglected field, there's brake to burn.   60
Consider now the lover and his love;
Whether their faults escape observance of
Each other, or if something rather frightful
In one, is in the other's eyes delightful.
A certain Balbus, so the story goes,   65
Loved even the polypus in Hagna's nose.
For friendship, I could wish we all would err,
Euphonious names on errors to confer.
Like father and son, we friends should never thus
For others' faults be too fastidious.   70
Coxey a father calls his son whose eyes
Are cocked; and for a son of pigmy size
The father calls him " Chick " like Sisyphus,
A formerly abortive little cuss.
Curley if knockkneed; one with wobbly walk   75
On rickety ankles " pa " in baby talk
Calls Rockefeller; so a man who's tight-
Fisted, if you call frugal, you'll be right;
If he's a silly ass who loudly brays
You'll call him free and easy in his ways;   80
If he's a blowhard, truculent of tongue,
Say he's plain-spoken, and you can't go wrong;
And if he has a temper hot as fire,
You only have to call him a live wire.
All this unites in friendship, as I guess,   85
And when united, serves that friendliness.
But we, — we turn the virtues upside down,
And daub a plate that's clean, a dirty brown.
A man who lives among us honestly

And does not strut his stuff continuously, 90
For us, his middle name is *slow* or *thick*.
And one who keeps from pitfalls and will pick
His way with care, and not expose his flank
To hostile stabs, knowing that life is rank
With many treacherous regions where foul deeds 95
And slanderous tongues spring up as thick as weeds,
Who sane and cautious, passes evil by,
We call him unreliable and sly.
And one is too straightforward, much like me,
Maecenas. This I got most frequently 100
From you, when I with thoughtless word or jest
Broke into a brown study. " He's a pest,"
We say, " and lacking certainly in tact."
Alas! how rashly all of us enact
Against ourselves, a harsh and unjust law. 105
Born without faults, there's none you ever saw.
The best of us are with the least of these
Beset. I want fair dealing, if you please.
Whatever may be best in me, dear friends,
May for my many failures, make amends; 110
And, if you'll have me love you, friend of mine,
I'd have you to my better self incline.
And so the right over the wrong prevails
If by that rule, weighed on the selfsame scales.
You and your wens, if you would not repel 115
A friend, be lenient with his warts as well.
Cherish forgiveness in your heart and mind
For others' faults, and you'll be paid in kind.
We come to wrath. With many failings more
It sticks inside a fool's interior. 120
You cannot cut it out in any wise.

Then why should Reason never utilize
Her weights and measures, fashioned with intent
To mete for various crimes due punishment?
A slave, when told to carry off a dish,   125
Laps up the sauce and leavings of the fish.
But if the master fixed him on a cross,
Serious men would not be at a loss
To call him crazier than Labeo.
But how much farther will your madness go,   130
And how much more will be your sinfulness
Against a friend who lightly may transgress?
If you forgive him not, you then may be
More than repulsive in severity.
Yet how you hate him and avoid his company!   135
As Ruso's debtor for a paltry sum,
Fled when he knew Black Monday soon would come.
If that poor beggar could not scrape the cash
Together somehow, he must go to smash;
And sit like captive with an outstretched throat,   140
And hear the awful histories Ruso wrote.
A friend may wet my couch when he is drunk;
Or from my table drop a piece of junk
Once handled by Evander; or a whole
Chicken may snitch out of my casserole;   145
He's hungry. But for this alone shall he
Be less of an agreeable friend to me?
What will I do, supposing he'd abscond
Or else betray a trust and jump his bond?

Those who are pleased to say all sins that are,   150
Will very nearly rate upon a par,

On Being Humane

Must strain themselves when they get down to facts.
Custom and commonsense will spurn such acts;
The Commonweal must hold them in despite,
Mother of almost all that's just and right.　　　155

When sentient creatures first crept out on Earth,
A dumb and lowdown flock were they at birth.
With nail or fist for nut and sleeping hole
They fought, and next with clubs. As onward roll
The years, with weapons fashioned for their need.　160
Next words and names that very well indeed
Will circumscribe sensations and ideas;
And then they leave off war; and next appears
A town which they will strongly fortify;
And then lay down the law; and by and by,　　　165
Burglar or brigand nobody shall be,
Nor anyone commit adultery.
Long before Helen, ages long before,
A quoniam was a cause for cruel war;
But all were unknown soldiers when they died,　　170
When, for a woman all could have beside
As beasts will couple in uncertain love,
A man who towered all the rest above,
Struck them all down, over them all preferred
Like some great bull, the leader of the herd.　　　175
The law was first invented, you'll confess,
For fear of rank injustice, more or less,
As you'll perceive if ever you unroll
History's chronicle upon the scroll.
For Nature of herself cannot be brought　　　　　180
To set apart whatever should be sought
From all to be avoided; to divide

Evil from good, may never so betide.
With Nature's aid alone, you cannot thus
Discern the upright from what's iniquitous.   185
Nor can you so prevail in Reason's name,
When you assert the sin must be the same
For one who in his neighbor's garden walks
To break young cabbages off from their stalks;
And one who, from a Temple's sacred shrine   190
Will steal by night the images divine.
There ought to be a rule and regulation
Inflicting punishment for every station.
For one who needs a whipping, who would urge
To cut him all to pieces with a scourge?   195
But never fear a stick for you will serve
'Gainst those who greater punishment deserve,
When you maintain that all things equal be,
From petty theft to highway robbery;
And when you threaten little crimes and great   200
Alike to whittle down and extirpate
With the same pruning knife for everything,
If men would only allow you to be king.
If Wisdom's always rich and handsome too,
And expert in the shaping of a shoe,   205
A king moreover, reverend and grave,
Why do you want what you already have?
" You fail to realize," he intervenes,
" Exactly what our sire Chrysippus means.
Said he: ' A wise man anything may be,   210
Even a shoemaker, though such as he
Need never stitch a boot nor cut a sole,
Nevertheless a cobbler sound and whole.' "
How so? " Hermogenes may songless keep

And yet in voice be top of all the heap 215
Known as an impresario far and wide;
Barber Alfenus may have laid aside
His implements of trade and shut up shop;
Yet for a haircut he will be the top.
So is a sage by acclamation made 220
A master workman, best in every trade.
Above all other men in everything,
And Reason thus proclaims him as a king."
But when you take a walk, it may be feared
Some naughty little boys will pull your beard; 225
And if you don't coerce them with your staff,
The crowd will hoot and hustle you and laugh.
With anger, you'll explode at such vile things,
And bark and howl, greatest of all great kings!
I'll cut it short. For very well, you know 230
When to a penny bath you sometimes go,
For all your royal progress, you have got
No retinue, unless that idiot
Crispinus follows after in your train.
Pardon, dear friends, I have not got a brain 235
Like his. If I occasionally make a break,
Why, I'll put up with any that you make.
I'll live a private citizen and be
So much more happy than his Majesty.

BOOK I

IV · How to Write Satire

Number Four may have been composed sometime in 39 B.C., before Horace became intimate with Maecenas, and after the public reading of poems had come into vogue with the opening of Pollio's public library.

Horace talks about his manner of writing and his conduct of life. The former he got from Aristotle and the latter from his father. It has been conjectured that the method of instruction employed by that keen and prudent intelligence really came from professors of philosophy and that Horace unconsciously mixed up his father's advice with the teachings of the Cynics. This theory seems pretty far-fetched. Why not take the words of Horace at their face value? The admonitions of his father are just what we should expect from the personal experience of a vigorous old man who has made his way in the world by dint of indefatigable industry, tact, and native shrewdness. Such sayings would naturally stick in the mind of the son. There is plenty of evidence that Horace had studied the works of various philosophers and that he often chose some of their doctrines to round out his father's instructions. There is also evidence that he took all the systems with a grain of salt. He adapted philosophy to his personal requirements, and not his personal requirements to philosophy.

In the *Satires* and *Epistles* Horace generally uses the plain style as against the grand style of Epic and Tragedy. In what he calls his metrical prose, he labors first of all to be clear and concise. He criticizes his prototype, Lucilius, for diffuseness and for muddy diction. He remarks that many of the verses ought to be deleted. Time has carried out his recommendation more fully than he intended. Of the *Satires* of Lucilius only a few scattered fragments remain. The principal use of these *disjecta membra* is for reconstruction by highly erudite persons in order to point out a source of inspiration for Horace's pedestrian muse.

Crispinus turns up again in this talk. He is Horace's *beau ideal* of what a philosopher and writer ought not to be — a windbag and a bore. He seems to have turned his system into verse and brought it out in book form. If so, he can hardly have rivalled Lucretius.

Talk Four

Cratinus, Eupolis, Aristophanes,
And other poets of old Comedies,
Anyone worth description used to tag
Because he was a thief and scalliwag,
Because he nabbed another fellow's wife,   5
Or tried to stick up people with a knife,
Or went notorious in some other way.
These they would drag into the light of day
And with the utmost freedom write them down.
On such Lucilius, for his renown,   10
Depended. Using different lines and feet
He followed them, their utterance to repeat.
Though keen of scent, with genial wit imbued,
The verses he composed were pretty crude;
For all his brilliance, he'd one fault to boot;   15
He would dictate while standing on one foot
Two hundred verses in a single hour
As evidence of great poetic power.
And full of mud his measures flow today
And many you would like to clear away.   20
Slipshod and garrulous, he took no pains;
For writing well he would not use his brains.
How large his output I'll not stop to say.

But look who's here! Crispinus comes our way
Ready to lay big odds upon a bet.   25

"Now if you care to take me up, I'll get
My notebook. Give me only time and place
And umpires, and I'll meet you face to face,
And who can write the most, we're going to see."
Surely the gods did very well by me, 30
Who made me with a scanty, timorous mind,
And few and far between, the words I find.
You, like a pair of goatskin bellows blow,
And out of you the windy noise may go
With pent-up blast to fan the laboring fire 35
And melt the iron, if you so desire.
Fortunate Fannius with his case of books!
From all the libraries, his portrait looks;
But no one reads the poems I indite;
I never dare in public to recite. 40
The reason why they do not like my style
Is just because they're mostly worth my while
For condemnation. Take out of a crowd
Whoever you would like to name aloud
For avarice vile, or one who'll always be 45
Agog for paltry popularity,
Or crazy after brides or after boys;
While one the sheen of silver overjoys,
And Albius is dotty on bronze; and one
Exchanges merchandise from rising sun 50
To where upon the evening of the day,
The region basks in slow departing ray.
Headlong he's borne through peril and through pain,
A cloud of dust, caught in a hurricane,
For fear he'll lose a little of his store, 55
Or else because he wants to make some more.
Of verse like this, they're all of them afraid,

And hate the poet, who the verses made.
"Don't you go near him. He has got the hay
Upon the horn! You'd better keep away!
If he can raise a laugh to gain his end,
There's no one he will spare, not even a friend.
And everything he scribbles on his sheets,
He foists on everybody that he meets,
Boys and old women, even as they come
From bakery or the pond, going back home."

Let's carry on with Reason for a guide
And get a little of the other side.
First from their number I acknowledge fit
To be called poets, I myself omit.
It's not enough to versify, you'd say;
A man who writes more nearly in the way
Of ordinary prose, you'll not regard
For all his finished verses, as a bard.
But one of inborn talent, with a mind
Beyond the mortal reach of humankind,
Whose tongue resounds with mighty songs of fame
Render to him the honor of that name.
And some have questioned whether Comedy
Can ever be considered poetry,
Since neither in dialogue nor situation
Is any force of ardent inspiration.
Except for regular poetic feet
That still recur, with measured rhythmic beat
The words and matter in no kind of way,
Differ from prose, plain talk of every day.
"But father's all burnt up, to ramp and rage
Over a prodigal son upon the stage.

A golddigger has driven him insane;
A wife with a big dowry he'll disdain;   90
Moreover, when he's drunk, he'll light a torch,
And paint the city red with wild debauch.
Long before night, he'll go out on a tear
And make a monstrous scandal everywhere."
But would Pomponius get a lighter licking,   95
If only father was alive and kicking?
It's therefore not enough with limpid word
Your smooth and fluent verses to record,
When, changed around in order, they'd be used
By anybody who a son accused,   100
His stomach heaving in the selfsame way
As raged the angry father in the play.
The words I write and those Lucilius wrote
Before me, out of measure if you quote,
Through all the forms and rhythms if you burst   105
And topsy-turvy put the last word first
And take the first and stick it on behind,
No trace of any poetry can you find.
But when you break this line of Ennius
In pieces; "After Discord hideous   110
Shattered the iron posts and gates of War,"
A poet's limbs are these, though scattered far
And wide. That's that. Another time we'll see
Whether or no the lines of Comedy
Are rightly poems. Now I ask you whether   115
In justice you're distrustful altogether
Of all that sort of writing. Sulcius
Is a keen sleuth; and so is Caprius.
And all around the town they run their course.
The voice of either snooper has grown hoarse   120

How to Write Satire

Accusing naughty men of what they do.
And both for grafters are a bugaboo.
A man whose hands are clean, his life exempt
From blame, can treat their libels with contempt.
If you, like Caelius, a thief may be
Or Birrius, why be afraid of me?
I'm not like Sulcius nor Caprius;
I'll never treat your peccadilloes thus;
No bookstore of my little books may boast;
My pages are not stuck up on a post;
No vulgar hand disfigures them with sweat;
Even Tigellius never makes them wet;
Never have I brought out a publication;
I never even gave a recitation,
Unless my friends have urged me here and there;
Otherwise, never openly, anywhere.
But many read aloud even in the public square,
Or in a public bath their verse they read;
Local acoustics there are fine indeed
And this amuses people void of sense
Incurious of an impertinence,
Who never question whether what you do
Were better done another time by you.
Some say: " You love to hurt, your vicious thought
Takes pleasure in it." Where can you have sought
For anything like this to throw at me?
Whom can you cite for your authority?
Anyone I have lived with? If a friend
In absence one backbites, or won't defend
When others blame him; anyone who tries
To get men's ribald laughter to uprise
And earn a reputation for a wit;

Or one who will a tale together fit
From what he has not seen, or who will not
Keep still about a confidence he's got,   155
A very shady customer is he.
Roman, beware of him! You'll often see
At dinner four apiece are parked on couches three
And one who with his wisecracks all has doused
Except the host and even him when soused;   160
And Liber, god of Truth, will make a start
To open up the secrets of the heart;
That man is full of fun for you, and free
And easy, and he seems good company,
Though shady characters you cannot bear.   165
But I who laugh in Folly's thoroughfare
At " Perfumes are Rufillus' meat. We note
His smell. Gargonius is like a goat,"
How can I seem by any kind of right
A lousy what's his name who likes to bite?   170
If in your presence, casual mention's made
Of how Petillius plied the burglar's trade
Upon the Capitol, you might defend
Him in your usual manner. He's my friend,
My dear companion up from boyhood's days: 175
I owe a lot to him in many ways;
I'm glad he lives in town without a fear
And yet I wonder how he got off clear."
Such is the very sepia of the squid,
Corroded rottenness that can't be hid.   180
May all my pages from this fault be free,
Also my soul. If anything by me
Were ever able to be promised true
This thing above all else, I promise you.

How to Write Satire

If with my language I am rather free 185
Or too jocose, I hope you'll pardon me,
And grant this privilege at my behest;
I got this habit from the very best
Of fathers; common failings so to shun
And mark examples down for everyone, 190
When he would urge me carefully to save,
So I could live content with what he gave;
" Look at the son of Albius, Baius too,
How wretchedly they live, how ill they do.
Here's an example eminent and great 195
Your patrimony not to dissipate."
When from the loves of a base paramour
He would dissuade me with paternal lore:
" Look at Scetanus. Surely you'd be quite
Dissimilar to him! his opposite! " 200
If I went after an adulteress
And I could have her bounty more or less:
" Trebonius got caught. Better think twice.
His reputation isn't very nice."
Said he: " Whatever is to seek or shun, 205
The highbrow gives you reasons thereupon,
But old tradition is enough for me.
If, while you need a guardian, I can see
You through, with life and reputation whole,
When manhood hardens you in body and soul, 210
And fashions into form your youthful fervor,
Why then, you'll swim without a life preserver."
So as a boy, he used to put me through
The sprouts; and so he told me what to do.
" Act thus and so. There's good authority." 215
Then for a model, he'd hold up for me

A member of the grand jury. If the lid
He put on me, some action to forbid:
"Why hesitate over what not to do?
This thing is very wrong, and useless too.   220
When so and so cut up in much the same
Way, what he did was called a burning shame."
As when a neighbor's funeral may scare
Sick gluttons, fear of death will make them spare
Themselves; so tender minds through others' blame   225
Will keep away from Vice in Virtue's name.
Immune am I to faults that may destroy,
But subject still to frailties that annoy;
Can you forgive me these which probably
Advancing years will take away from me,   230
Or candid friends, or even my own intent,
When with myself I have an argument?
Absorbed in portico or easy chair
I never leave myself. I'm still right there.
"Is this the better way?" "If I do this   235
The life I lead, will seldom go amiss."
"This way I'll meet desirable friends."
"This simply is not done; it so offends.
Could ever I act so imprudently?"
With screwed up lips, I thus commune with me,   240
And put the question. In a leisure moment
On paper I'll jot down my playful comment.
A swarm of bards are my auxiliary.
For we are in the great majority.
We'll raise the roof with propaganda loud   245
Just like the Jews; and make you join our crowd.

BOOK I

V · THE JOURNEY

TALK FIVE has been freely and charmingly translated by Cowper. It may have been composed either in 38 or 37 B.C. We only know for certain that it describes the route of an embassy sent to Antony by Octavian and that it was not the first which he sent. The Second Triumvirate was then in full bloom and dissensions between Octavian and Antony had got under way. Of these the little friend of Maecenas gives only a very gentle hint. Horace never wears his politics upon his sleeve.

Some critics maintain that the *Sermo* is merely of antiquarian interest, because Horace does not describe the route vividly, but confines himself to such details as that the water was bad at one place and the bread was good at another. Why then should it have continued to amuse posterity and why should Cowper have deemed it worth translating? It seems to me that such critics are finding fault with the *Sermo* for what it is not. It is not intended to be a panorama of natural beauties. It is a journal of a trip, and it is modeled on a similar journal from the facile pen of Lucilius. Like many of the *Sermones*, it was probably meant to be read aloud, possibly to divert some of the people who actually went on the journey. The lively scenes on the canal boat, the slapstick encounter of the two buffoons, and a number of other incidents are calculated to raise a laugh.

One fancies a dinner given by Maecenas sometime after

his return from Athens on his second embassy. Varius and Virgil may have been among those present, and Cocceius and Fonteius Capito. As the guests linger over their apples and wine, Maecenas announces that Horace has written an entertaining little skit about their journey to Brundisium — no politics, no headaches, just friendliness and fun. So they laugh over the reminiscences of the journey, and Horace is applauded, and gratified at such applause.

At the end there is a passage adapted from Lucretius and Epicurus — how the gods have nothing to do with human affairs, so that everything that happens on earth is a natural phenomenon and never a miracle, whatever the Jews might say. Was Horace in earnest when he wrote like this? If so, his views were not widely divergent from those of Huxley and Herbert Spencer. How does such skepticism accord with his Odes where he urges the Romans to consider themselves less than the gods?

I think that the Talk was meant for an intimate circle and at least some of the Odes for a larger audience. Men like Maecenas and Augustus probably harbored pretty radical personal opinions and yet believed that Roman tradition and Roman religion should be upheld for the sake of Roman morale. Is such an attitude insincere? Possibly, to a New England conscience. But it was adopted by such respectable members of society as Matthew Arnold and Montaigne. I doubt if Augustus really considered himself a god, any more than the King of Great Britain and Northern Ireland really thinks of himself as an Episcopalian when he is in England and a Presbyterian when he is in Scotland. The ideas of Maecenas and his friends were their own; and they evidently talked them over among themselves and did not believe that incense was melted by supernatural means, either at Egnatia or anywhere else. There are people in the world today who do not hail as a miracle the liquefaction of the blood of St. Januarius. It is the same thing over again in the same region.

Talk Five

From mighty Rome, my travels I begin;
A cheap Arician roadhouse takes me in;
Heliodorus was my company;
Head of a school of rhetoric was he,
And very widely read in Grecian lore.
Thence to Appian market, one day more,
Cram full of tars and publicans who cheat
You out of your eye teeth; our laggard feet
Had made us twice as long upon our way;
A hiker in his togs takes but one day.
More slowly if you pace the Appian road,
Your journey will not be so grave a load.
Tummy and I a state of war declared;
The water was so very vilely bad.
I hardly could get settled in my mind,
To wait for my companions, while they dined.
Night with her shadows now had clothed the Earth;
In spangled skies her signs she marshalled forth.
When slave on sailor heaped a clamorous din
And sailor and slave. "Gangway! You've planted in
Three hundred!" "All aboard!" "Enough now there!"
They hitched the mule and then took up the fare
And one whole hour went by. Out of the bogs
The damnable mosquitoes and the frogs
Chased away sleep. A sailor pretty soused

With booze, about his girl friend loud caroused;
"The girl I left behind me," was the strain;
A man on board came in for the refrain.
That man at last got tired and shut his eyes.
Then with a rope the lazy boatman ties 30
The mule up to a rock and lets him graze.
And down upon his back himself he lays
And snores; and even at the dawn of day
We had not felt the boat get underway,
Till one of us who had a headstrong mind 35
Jumped out and on the head and the behind
Lambasted mule and sailor with a stick
Of willow very flexible and thick.
At last by ten we barely get to land;
In your clear rill, Feronia, wash the hand 40
And face; and after breakfast creep along
Three miles; till Anxur highly placed among
White rocks upon her headland gleams afar.
Here noble Maecenas and Cocceius are
To come as legates, great occasion sends, 45
Each an old hand at settling strife of friends.
With black collyrium here I rubbed sore eyes.
Meanwhile arrives Maecenas with the wise
Cocceius and Fonteius Capito,
A highly finished gentleman, you know. 50
He was upon the side of Antony
And no one else a greater friend than he.
Now to the town of Fundi we had come,
Its praetor and its grand panjandarum,
Aufidius Luscus. We were very glad 55
To leave, for we were laughing so like mad
At all the decorations he possessed,

The Journey

Once an amanuensis, now all dressed
In senatorial toga. What a man!
Broad purple stripe and charcoal in a pan
For incense burning, which a slave before
Him in his pompous progress proudly bore.
Mamurra's city wearily we gained
And overnight we all of us remained;
Murena furnished quarters neat and clean;
And Capito looked after the cuisine.
Most grateful was the morrow's light to greet
At Sinuessa; here we were to meet
Plotius and Varius and Vergilius.
Earth never bore three souls more gracious.
Three whiter men I never look to see
And no one else more clearly bound to me.
O the embraces! What rejoicings there!
I never matched such transports anywhere!
While I'm in my right mind, nothing can lend
Such bliss as a companionable friend.
Near the Campanian bridge a little shack
Gave us a roof which otherwise we'd lack;
Here overnight our party made a halt
And greeters had to furnish wood and salt.
Next day in Capua, the mules set down
Our luggage; in good time we made that town.
And here Maecenas to the ball game went;
Virgil and I were readily content
To get a snooze. We felt that playing ball
Was hostile to sore eyes and stomachs all
Upset. Cocceius later was to bring
Us to his villa full of everything,
High up above the inns of Caudium.

Full fain am I, O Muse, for you to come 90
For me, that I commemorate short and soon
The combat of Sarmentus the buffoon
And Messius Cicirrus; how they oppose
Each other; from what parents each arose.
From famous Oscan forebears Messius sprung; 95
Now of Sarmentus let the song be sung;
The noble dame who owned him as a slave
In former days, not yet has reached her grave.
Sarmentus first: " You're certainly a wild horse! "
We get a laugh. Quoth Messius: " Why, of course 100
I'm with you." And he pivoted his head
About; and right away Sarmentus said:
" O ho! You must be quite some unicorn
I do not think. But where would be your horn?
Without the amputation on the brow 105
What would you do, if so you threaten now? "
For his disfigurement, a scar was cleft
Along his fuzzy forehead on the left.
Rather too much we gave his face the bird:
" Campanian disease " was all the word. 110
He asked if we should like to have him dance;
Like any pastoral Cyclops he could prance.
No need of mask nor tragedy's high heel.
Cicirrus talked about it a good deal.
And lit into Sarmentus once again. 115
" Your household gods had ought to get a chain
When on their altars you should make a vow.
Being a clerk can't help you anyhow.
Your owner's got the law on you today."
He asked him how he came to run away. 120
A pound of meal would more than stuff his skin,

The Journey

The measly insect was so dreadful thin.
That supper kept right on with merriment.
Next day we straight to Beneventum went.
Our host was just a trifle overdiligent.   125
While turning skinny thrushes on a spit,
He nearly burnt himself and all his kit.
In that old kitchen, far from fireproof,
Voracious Vulcan almost licked the roof.
The hungry guests snatched up their evening meal,   130
Also the slaves who trembled a great deal;
Then might you see how all together turned
To quench the conflagration as it burned.
Apulia henceforth began to show
Her summits; well the sight of them I know.   135
Atabulus' hot blasts her mountains parch.
We wavering slowly on our forward march,
Could never so have scaled them, as to win
Our way, unless a farm had taken us in.
Trivicum was in the vicinity.   140
A smoky stove brough tears to every eye,
Burning wet leaves and logs as green as grass.
And here I made a most consummate ass
Out of myself. Right up to midnight I
Wait for a wench who fooled me with a lie;   145
For love I was keyed up. Till far away
By slumber borne, upon my back I lay.
And so a naughty vision did me dirt.
It wet my stomach and it stained my shirt.
Hence four and twenty miles we swiftly sped   150
Onward in coaches, till we made our bed
Within a tiny village. In such verse
As these its name I cannot well rehearse.

It won't fit in. But with a certain sign
That town I very easily define.　　　　　　155
The water, cheap elsewhere, they sell instead.
But here they bake the very loveliest bread;
So a smart man shoulders a load of it
Upon his way; for bread is full of grit
When to Canusium your steps you turn,　　160
With water no more plenty by an urn.
Canusium was founded ages since
By Diomed, the valiant Grecian prince.
And here for Varius the journey ends,
And sadly he departs from grieving friends.　　165
At Rubi next arrives our weary train,
Long was the road we took, made worse by rain.
The weather then grew better; worse the road
Straight up to Bari's walls, the famed abode
Of fish. Then Gnatia, built beneath the ire　　170
Of water nymphs. Incense without a fire
They melted in the temple's outer court.
They wanted us to credit that report.
They made us laugh; some jokes were also made;
And still they were desirous to persuade.　　175
The Jew Apella may believe, not I.
For I have learned eternal and on high
The gods lead lives exempt from mortal care.
Marvels are Nature's deeds, however rare.
Never will gods from lowering heaven's high roof　　180
Send any portent down for our behoof.
Brundisium is the limit of my song,
Long was the way, even as the tale is long.

BOOK I

VI · Horace and his Father

This might be called an epistle. It may have been written to Maecenas in the first flush of enthusiasm for the newly acquired friendship. But even the first flush of enthusiasm did not make Horace lose his self-respect. It is a manly tribute, free from any suspicion of servility. It is modeled somewhat on Lucilius, and follows the order prescribed by Greek rhetoricians, namely, race, upbringing, training, education, growth of mind and body, profession and practice.

Horace here preaches moderation not only in thought, but in conduct of life. He prefers worth to birth, but disclaims any ambition for a public career and pokes fun at social and political climbers. He has little use for city politics, because the aspirants for office make high-sounding promises which they cannot keep, and because the Roman voters are excitable, fickle, and abusive, and are entirely dominated by a big name and a big noise. What a contrast to the disinterested sagacity of our political leaders and our sane and sober electorate!

Talk Six

OF ALL the dwellers on Etruscan ground
For somewhat Lydian ancestry renowned,
Maecenas, if we give to each his due,
There is no greater gentleman than you.
Though on maternal and paternal side 5
Your grandsires mighty legions used to guide,
Unlike the common run, a squinnied nose
You never will turn up at any of those
Whose forebears were unknown, nor even at me
Born of a father who had been set free. 10
A man must be freeborn, but otherwise
You don't go in for genealogies;
And what his father was, won't interest you.
You'll therefore be convinced that this is true;
Long years before the distant day and hour 15
When Tullius had come to regal power
Whose mother was a slave of low degree,
Many a man without much ancestry,
Leading a life of probity and worth,
Won ample honors, that belied his birth. 20
Laevinus, on the other hand, come down
From that Valerius of old renown
Who banished from the realm, Tarquin the Proud,
Could never, as the many have allowed,
Be any more expensive than one cent. 25

Horace and his Father

Voters, you know, are not intelligent.
Honors they give to men who have no merit,
The servile fools of halfwits who inherit
Titles, or whose patrician galleries
Are lined with forebears' waxen effigies.   30
What part is proper then for us to play,
From all the vulgar herd so far away?
Only suppose the populace prefer
Such honors on Laevinus to confer
While Decius, the parvenu, they flout.   35
Suppose the censor moved to kick me out,
And I must be held up to public scorn
Because I had a father not freeborn.
I'd sure deserve the jam that I got in,
Not staying put inside of my own skin.   40
Forever chained to Glory's glittering car
Alike the vulgar and the nobles are.
So Tillius, what's the use, when yesterday
Your senatorial stripe was torn away,
To seek a tribune's office to attain,   45
So you can wear the purple once again?
Malicious envy only grows more rife,
Much less, if you retired to private life.
Who wants to stand in senatorial shoes
Is crazy; that will be his sole excuse,   50
When with black leather thongs his legs are dressed,
And broad the stripe let down upon his chest;
Continually he'll hear: "Who is that man?
Who was his father?" Barrus once began
To be infected with a strange disease;   55
And with a splendid shape desired to please.
Wherever he went the girls would then and there

Look over all his points with interest rare,
And ask about his face, calves, feet and teeth and hair.
So if a man will make a promise to 60
The voters, of big things that he will do
For City, Empire, Italy and the shrine
Of every god the Romans hold divine,
Those mortals all are bound to ask with care:
" Who was his father? Was the lady fair 65
Who bore him, flesh of flesh and bone of bone,
A woman no one else had ever known?
How dare you, son of a Syrus or a Damas
Or of a Dionysus, so to shame us?
Would you a Roman citizen throw down 70
From the Tarpeian Rock, you base born clown?
Or hand to Cadmus to be executed? "
" But Novius, my colleague so reputed,
Must park one seat behind me, when we see
The games. He's what my father used to be." 75
" And so you think yourself on this account
A Paulus or Messalla? What do you amount
To anyway? But he's the people's choice.
Novius has a mighty speaking voice.
For when two hundred trucks make an infernal
 noise, 80
And three large funerals come to swell the sound
In the great Forum, louder he'll resound;
Trumpets and horns alike his voice will drown.
Anyway, we're not going to let him down."
So now I will return again to me, 85
" Born of a father who had been set free."
Like rats they gnaw me, every slanderous knave,
" Born of a father who had been a slave."

Horace and his Father

And that's the way they now behave to me,
Maecenas, when we both good comrades be; 90
And that's the same old argument they made
Because a Roman legion once obeyed
Me for a Colonel, maybe rightly then;
But now I'll say it's something else again.
My former honor, all the world agrees 95
Could give a grouch to anyone you please.
But why should anyone be jealous now
Of you and me as friends; they must know how
Particular you are in making friends
Only of those with worthy aims and ends; 100
All base and crooked flattery is far
From you, who pick your friends for what they are.
So for our friendship, I could never say
Only a stroke of luck had come my way.
No happy chance bestowed you upon me, 105
But Virgil once, and best of all was he.
After him Varius; so it came to pass
When they had told you everything I was.
But when I came before you, face to face,
I hemmed and hawed, much to my own disgrace. 110
Like a small infant bashfully I came,
And more I could not say for very shame.
Not I a father's fame inherited;
I never rode upon a thoroughbred
Across the Satureian countryside; 115
I told you what I was; and you replied
Little, for that's your way; and off I pack.
And when nine months went by, you called me back,
And bade me to be numbered with your friends;
And this, I reckon, all the rest transcends, 120

That I should be found pleasing in your sight,
With your discernment of the wrong and right.
Me no paternal honors recommend;
But pure in life and heart, I am your friend.
And if my blemishes are slight and few, 125
But otherwise I'm naturally true,
As for a body shapely on the whole,
You might pick flaws, if spotted by a mole,
If none could really blame me to my hurt
For greed or any other kind of dirt, 130
If to a fancy house I never went,
But all my life was pure and innocent,
If I do say so, and to friends endeared,
My father was the reason. So he reared
Me. Poor he was. His paltry little field 135
Could scarcely a sufficient harvest yield;
Yet he refused to put me in the rule
Of Flavius, who ran the village school;
Where boys of big centurions used to go.
Big husky boys; who carried to and fro 140
On the left arm, the satchel and the slate.
The middle of each month, they shelled out eight
Coppers for payment. But my father dared
To bring his boy to Rome to be prepared,
A training any senator or knight 145
Would give his sons, if they were taught aright.
My dress, the slaves who followed me about,
If one could notice me in all that rout,
He'd think the pomp and circumstance was due
Alone to large ancestral revenue. 150
Father himself acted as bodyguard,
Not to be bribed by any man's reward.

He went to my instructors every day
About the school. There is no more to say.
Honorably my father saved for me
The flower of all the virtues, chastity,
Not only in the fact but in the name.
On me no breath of scandal ever came;
He never was afraid of anyone
Who told him he did wrong to give his son
A liberal education. Even if I
Earned but an auctioneer's small salary,
Or if a bill collector I'd remain,
As he was once, I never could complain.
For all this now, what praise can I bestow
On him, much greater than the thanks I owe?
Could I of such a father be inclined
Ever to be ashamed, in my right mind?
Some think they're smart, saying they're not to blame
For parents who had neither name nor fame.
I'll not defend myself in any way
Like that; and what I think and what I say
Will nothing have in common with that crowd.
If, after certain years had been allowed,
At Nature's call, we lived them over again
And other parents of a nobler strain
Each could select according to desire,
Whomever his ambition might require,
Such high and haughty honors I'd resign,
Content with what in former days were mine.
The crowd will call me crazy; you, maybe,
Pronounce me sane, when for the like of me
The fasces I refuse, and curule chair, —
Such crushing burdens, all unfit to bear.

If I desired to take a rustic trip   185
All by myself, I never more could slip
Out of the city. I should have to feed
A train of grooms and thoroughbreds. I'd need
A coach. But now, according to my due
I take a bobtailed mule for retinue.   190
And way down to Tarentum I can go
With him. My saddle bags will chafe below
His buttocks, while his rider sore must gall
His foreparts. But there's nobody to call
Me stingy, Tillius, as the gossips goad   195
You when you travel the Tiburtine road.
A praetor very niggardly behaves
Who on a journey only takes five slaves,
To carry for the hour when he would dine
A portable oven and a hamper of wine.   200
In that and in a thousand other ways,
Your Excellency, I can pass my days
Much more agreeably than you have done.
Whenever I want, I take a walk alone.
I bargain over cabbages and flour;   205
I ramble round the Circus at the hour
Of evening, where they gyp the people so;
And afterwards around the Forum go;
At fortune teller's booths I show my hand;
And last of all, once more at home I land.   210
Arrived I sup on scallions, potted pease
And pancakes made of meal and fried in grease;
Three boys will wait on me; a slab of white
Marble upholds two cups of measure right
For mixing of the water and the wine.   215
An inexpensive saltcellar is mine;

Pitcher and plate to pour libations there,
And both are of Campanian earthenware.
And so to bed, where worry dies aborning.
I need not get up early in the morning   220
To plead my clients' cases and to see
Marsyas' statue glowering down at me;
Inside the Forum; always frowning thus,
His face abhors the junior Novius
Who just behind his back a pawnshop keeps,   225
Open for business, while the city sleeps.
I'm up at ten to take a little walk,
Or read or write with no disturbing talk.
A rubdown then with olive oil, not that
Stolen from table lamps by nasty Nat;   230
And when the sun with penetrating rays
Reminds me to the bath to go my ways,
I keep away from Campus and the ball
Game. Afterwards my lunch is very small,
An empty stomach just enough to stay.   235
And so at home I pass the time away.
Desire for honor and the heavy strife
Of fell ambition cumber not my life;
But cheerfully I live and at my ease.
In such a life there is much more to please   240
Than if a quaestor grandfather were mine,
And father and my uncle all in line.

BOOK I

VII · THE PUN

THIS talk is what the Greeks called a *chreia*, or pointed anecdote, leading up to a quaint action or a *bon mot*. So far as I know, it is the earliest satire extant. It may have been written at Rome shortly after Philippi. But the reference to Brutus as overlord of the Asian wealth could hardly have been acceptable to the anticaesarians, inasmuch as it was common gossip that the distinguished patriot in question had exacted 48 per cent interest on a loan to the Saliminians and refused payment of the principal, because he liked the investment so well.

The pun at the end seems to some scholars the sole *raison d'être* for an immature piece of work. But I like to think that Maecenas and his coterie enjoyed the Talk, both for its mock heroics, and for the lively portrayal of two very ridiculous characters. The work may be immature, but it reveals great dramatic power and the Horatian flair for vivid description in miniature.

Talk Seven

How Persius, the half breed, once for all
Wrought vengeance on Rupilius King his gall,
The outlaw, still I think may be of note
As barber's or beautician's anecdote.
This Persius was rich; a magnate he 5
With major interests at Clazomenae,
And loathsome litigation with this King.
Hard boiled, his every word would scorch and sting;
He was the more obstreperous of the two;
His cussedness could even King outdo, 10
Puffed up with self-importance and conceit.
They say white horses have the speediest feet,
White horses he could distance in the race,
Though Barrus and Sisena set the pace.
Now back again to King once more I go, 15
Neither would come to terms with either foe;
These troublemakers claim a hero's right
To meet the enemy in adverse fight.
'Twixt Hector, son of Priam all afire,
And great Achilles, was ferocious ire 20
Till Death did finally depart the twain.
No other cause impelled them to their bane
Than Valor which in each was overall.
But if vexatious Discord may befall
Poltroons, or if a war unequal prove 25

The Pun

As Diomed with Lycian Glaucus strove,
The weaker will decamp and gifts will send;
So may a coward be a foeman's friend.
When Brutus ruled the Asian wealth out there,
Rupilius and Persius were a pair.   30
No better was the gladiatorial might
Of Bacchius and Bithus for a fight;
Up to the bar, ferociously they charge;
And either as a spectacle loomed large.
Persius presents his case; the audience laugh.   35
He eulogizes Brutus and his staff;
Brutus the Sun of Asia, he must call;
Around about him in the courtroom, all
His comrades lesser luminaries are,
Each in his place a most salubrious star,   40
Except for King. The Dog-star was that bum,
A blight and evil omen he had come;
A hateful constellation boding harm
For anyone who ever tilled a farm.
On, on he roared as foams a winter stream   45
Whose waters rarely catch the hatchet's gleam
In wild ravine or tangled mountain glen.
It was the turn of the Praenestian then.
He cursed and swore like guys who gather grapes;
Against our laughter from his mouth escapes   50
A very bitter current of hot air;
You could not beat him, tough beyond compare,
As one who tardily his vines may trim;
A passerby will give the bird to him,
Crying out loud "Cuckoo! you're pruning late!"   55
And then is beaten up with billingsgate.
As Grecian Persius stood before the bar,

All wet with that Italian vinegar
He raised his voice: " By the great gods I pray
You, Brutus! Ain't it your accustomed way   60
To ruin royalty? Why don't you now
Cut this King's throat. That is your job and how! "

BOOK I

VIII · PRIAPUS AND WITCHES

For the macabre soliloquy of the garden god I know of no closer parallel than *Tam o' Shanter*. Both Horace and Burns pile up "mair of horrible and awefu'," till they end by being funny. Like the fat boy in Pickwick, they " wants to make your flesh creep."

It is an unconscious tribute to genius that commentators from Porphyrio down, have proved to their own satisfaction that Horace was once under the spell of Canidia, or Gratidia, a Neapolitan vendor of perfumes, that she " done him wrong," and that he vilified her in revenge. I confess that this exegesis seems to me as ridiculous as if we supposed that Nanny had treated Burns badly and was, in consequence, put into *Tam o' Shanter*. As a matter of fact, there is no evidence of the existence of Canidia outside of the works of Horace. There is nothing to show that she might not have been a creation of his own — a composite of what he had observed in his evening strolls about the Forum and the Circus Maximus, where he conversed with fortune tellers and other fakirs. Be that as it may, Canidia dwells at present in the Land of Fiction, with Ariosto's *Bella Alcina*, Tasso's *Insidiosa Armida*, the false Duessa of Edmund Spenser, and Nanny and her cutty sark. Canidia is as real as Meg Merriles, so real that the literally minded must needs gossip about her and her creator.

Personally, I do not believe that Horace had any more

faith in witchcraft than he had in miracles; and I think his enlightened skepticism was shared by his friends. Maecenas showed what he thought of superstition by taking the graveyard on the "black Esquiline," and making it over into a garden and building a villa on the hilltop. But he disapproved of the practice of sorcery because of its morbid effect on ignorant credulity. Possibly he and Horace talked the matter over, and this Priapea was the outcome. Some years later Agrippa, the coadjutor of Maecenas, endeavored to drive the witches and warlocks out of Rome; and perhaps he found out that you cannot put down superstition by force. I fancy that Horace's ridicule was more effective.

Talk Eight has made many echoes in English, — in Middleton's *Witch*, for instance, and more portentously, in those tremendous scenes where the weird sisters on the blasted heath beguile and betray Macbeth to his doom.

Talk Eight

Once on a time, I was a fig tree trunk,
Only a log of wood and piece of junk;
The cabinet maker, in a quandary
Whether to make a ladder out of me
Or a Priapus, rather thought he'd try   5
To make a god; and so a god am I.
Robbers and birds in terror of me stand;
A sickle for the yeggs in my right hand
Will put the fear of god in each low soul;
As also from lewd groin, my long red pole.   10
Firm on my topknot sits a reedy crown
To scare ill-mannered birds from settling down;
In this new park, I'll be their prohibition;
But formerly a slave of vile condition
Would pay to have dead comrades carried here,   15
From their poor shacks, thrown out on a cheap bier.
Here was the paupers' common burial lot;
Pantolabus the clown is on the spot;
The spendthrift Nomentanus, here he lies;
And there's a post to mark the boundaries,   20
Frontage a thousand feet, three hundred deep;
No heirs at law may any title keep
To that memorial in anyways,
So graven on the stone with legal phrase.
Now it is healthy on the Esquiline   25

To live; and if the weather might be fine,
To stroll along the sunny old earth wall
Where Melancholy once reigned over all,
Where in a grisly field, instead of stones,
You only looked at piles of whitening bones.   30
Worry and toil come not so much for me
From prowlers and wild creatures that I see,
Who now habitually infest the place,
As those with charms and drugs of evil grace
To overturn a human being's mind.   35
No sort of an expedient could I find
To stop them, or their practices confound.
When the full moon, who roams her orbit round,
Decorously uplifts a lovely face,
They gather noxious herbs about the place,   40
And bones they snatch; and I myself did see
Canidia with black robe above her knee
Run with dishevelled locks; her feet were bare;
With her old Sagana was howling there;
Their nails scratch up the earth; they, with their teeth,   45
Tear a black lamb to pieces; and beneath
Into the ditch the clotted blood drips red,
To conjure up the spirits of the dead;
And every shade, responsive to that spell
Whatever they inquire, is bound to tell.   50
Two images were near the bloody pool,
One wool, one wax; the larger was of wool;
And on the smaller, punishment impelled.
Even as one to supplication quelled,
Stood the wax image, like an abject slave   55
Soon to be sent in torment to the grave.

Priapus and Witches

One called on Hecate, and one the dire
Tisiphone, her presence to require;
Right up from Hell, the hounds and serpents rush.
The moon at such a sight was all ablush.   60
Such doings never should be seen by her;
She hid behind a great big sepulchre;
If there is any lie in what I've said,
May ravens leave white droppings on my head;
Julius and Crook Voranus on me squirt,   65
And fairy Pediatia do me dirt!
Such details why should I enumerate,
How Sagana's antiphones alternate
With ghostly voices gibbering sad and shrill;
Who answered her according to her will;   70
How stealthy in the ground a hole they make
For beard of wolf and tooth of spotted snake;
And how the blaze was ever spurting higher
As soon as the wax image fed the fire.
The din those Furies make, the deeds they do   75
Gave me the horrors as I watched the two.
But at the last I managed to get back
At them; like bursting bladder came the crack
I made, that split the wood upon the rump.
Back to the city, both the witches jump.   80
Canidia's teeth exploded with a cough;
Sagana's haughty headpiece toppled off;
And all their herbs, their loveknots and their charms
Were cast down on the pathway from their arms.
As off they ran in ignominious rout,   85
You'd see stupendous jokes to laugh about.

BOOK I

IX · THE PEST

"THE PEST" seems to have been modeled on a satire of Lucilius, but it may have been taken from personal experience as well. The hero has been called "the bore" by many scholars; but this particular bore not only bored but pestered. During the lively dialogue between Horace and his persecutor, we get a pleasant picture of the disinterested relationship between Maecenas and his friends.

Talk Nine has always been a favorite. In France, the theme was used by Molière in "Les Fâcheux," which was presented before Louis XIV and his Court at the Palais Royal in 1661. More than a half century before, in the reign of Henry IV, Regnier had used it in his Eighth Satire. In England contemporaneously with Molière it was used by Dr. Donne in Satire Number One. In 1759 it was brought up to date in a free translation by William Cowper. But long before either of the two, it had been staged by Ben Jonson in the *Poetaster* (1601) — a drama, by the bye, where Horace appears, together with Maecenas and his coterie. Several characters in the Talks also tread the boards — Hermogenes Tigellius, for example, who acts out what Horace says of him at the beginning of Talk Three, and Crispinus, whom Ben has made into the bore himself. How much other bores of other authors owe to this sprightly dialogue is something for some fellar to find out. We know that Thackeray was a confirmed Horatian. Is it too much to suppose that the Mulligan in Mr. Perkins' Ball could trace back his lineage not only to Irish kings, but to the enterprising and talkative individual who has been anonymously immortalized by Horace?

Talk Nine

I strolled along the sacred Boulevard
Pondering a wisecrack for its own reward,
All wrapped up in my verses. When there came
A man I really only knew by name
And gripped my hand. "My dear old top," said he,   5
"How goes it?" " Well enough as now things be.
I trust that everything goes well with you."
And when I turned away, he stuck like glue.
Said I, "There's something else you want with me?"
"You ought to know me better," answered he.   10
"I'm very highly cultured." "That means more
Than what you let me see of you before."
Desperately I desired to get away;
I hurry up, and then I stand at bay
And in my servant's ear whisper appeals,   15
While perspiration runs down to my heels.
"Bolanus, you're in luck that you have got
A head that like your temper's, always hot,"
I muttered, while he talked and showed no pity.
He blurbed about the beauties of the city.   20
And when I answered nothing: "It's hard luck!
I've noticed all along you want to duck;
You can't shake me, you know; I've got you now.
Where are you going? I'll follow anyhow."
"You need not run around in circles so.   25

The Pest

The man I'm going to see, you do not know.
He lives across the Tiber a long way,
Near Caesar's gardens and he's sick today."
" Well, well, there's nothing much round here to do
And I am keen. I'll go along with you."   30
I lower my ears like an ill-tempered ass
Upon whose back the heavy burdens mass.
" If you but knew me well," so he began,
" Varius or Viscus were no better man
For friend of yours. For who could ever be   35
So quick and copious with his poetry,
Or who can shake a leg in any dance
With sex appeal to melt you with romance?
And when I sing, I never fail to please
Even to the envy of Hermogenes."   40
Here seemed to be a chance to stop this bother.
" You might catch something. Haven't you a mother
Or relative who needs you safe and sound? "
" Nobody now. I've put them underground."
" God rest their souls! Behold the hour draws near 45
To finish off with me, for I'm still here.
An aged Sabine sorceress sang a song
For me in other days when I was young.
This lot for me she drew to serve my turn
When she had shaken her prophetic urn.   50
And now sad fate has overtaken me,
Now the full meaning of the words I see:
'Nor poison nor the sword will put you out
Pneumonia, consumption nor slow gout;
Someday a blatant bore will be your fate.   55
Avoid him when you come to man's estate.' "
We reached the spot a little after nine

Where Vesta's temple and the court combine.
That morning he's been summoned to the place
And if he didn't appear, he'd lose his case.   60
" If you like me one little bit," said he,
" Help me this once and come and vouch for me."
" You know where I am going," so said I,
" And damned if I can help you if I try.
I'm the worst witness any ever saw;   65
I don't know anything about the law."
Said he, " I have my doubts on what to do
Whether I'd better quit the case or you."
" Me, by all means," said I. Said he, " Nay! nay! "
And pronto he proceeds to lead the way.   70
To match yourself against a champion
Is never easy, and I followed on.
" How do you and Maecenas get along? "
So he began again: " His mind is strong
And very few his intimates must be,   75
And none has used good luck more dextrously.
Now if a certain man you'd introduce
He'll help you out. You'll find him of great use
Against the rest. I'm damned if you would not
With him along, get rid of the whole lot."   80
" We do not live there in the kind of way
You seem to think, from what I hear you say.
There is no cleaner house nor any more
Averse to intrigue when you pass the door,"
Said I. " But everybody has his place.   85
As for myself I count it no disgrace,
If one with coin or brains surpasses me."
" That's great, but hardly credible," said he.
" But that's the way it is." " You make me more

Anxious to get right next him than before." 90
" You only have to wish and with your pluck
Over the top you'll go with best of luck.
It's more than easy to beat down his guard.
That's why the first approaches are so hard."
" He'll never get me down. His slaves I'll pay 95
With tips; and if they kick me out today
Tomorrow I'll be back. I'll get him there
Or on the boulevard or public square.
' Naught without toil can Life to mortals lend.' "
While this kept on and on, an intimate friend, 100
Fuscus Aristius, here hove in sight.
Down to the ground he knew that fellow right.
Both of us stopped to pass the time of day.
" Where are you coming from, and whither away? "
I tried to nab him by the coat. My fist 105
Only enclosed a very lifeless wrist.
I nod and wink for rescue. All the while
The cutup smiled a most deceptive smile;
That burned me up. " You said most certainly
You'd private matters to discuss with me." 110
" Yes, I remember. At a fitting season
Will you and I about those matters reason.
Today's Yom Kippur. Even you'd refuse
To thumb the nose at circumcised Jews."
" I'm not a superstitious man," I say, 115
" Nor share in their beliefs in any way."
" Well, as for me, I'm just a little yellow
About their rites. I'm a peculiar fellow
And all their superstitions I allow.
Another time I'll talk. Excuse me now." 120
I'll tell the world the sun grew black for me.

That rascal ran away and let me be
Under the knife. The plaintiff in the case
Now came on his opponent face to face.
" O there you are. You miserable cur! 125
And you, you'll act as witness, my dear sir? "
With right good will I offer him my ear
To touch and as a witness to appear,
The customary sign. As with a claw,
He grips his man in clutches of the law. 130
There's a great noise and running round about.
And that's the way Apollo helped me out.

BOOK I

X · POETIC CLIQUES

Talk Ten was evidently composed after the preceding talks, — possibly in 35 B.C., when Horace had decided to publish his first volume. Like the rest, its emphasis is brought out by reading aloud. I should not wonder if Horace actually read it to some of the friends whom he mentions at the finish. There are twelve in all, and they could have been readily accommodated at one time at Maecenas' dining table, or tables.

The Talk deals with literary dissensions long since past and gone. There may have been some politics mixed in, but Horace does not mention them. From him and others we learn that at this time there were several literary cliques in Rome. There were the Alexandrians, the followers of Calvus and Catullus, the " modern poets " as they were called. Catullus still delights us; but of the rest scarcely a vestige remains, for " modernity " in poetry is usually transient. Some of them seem to have wanted to enlarge the Latin language by coining new words from the Greek. There were also the upholders of the old order, partisans of the old Latin poets in general and of Lucilius in particular, whose niece had married Pompey, — people who resented criticism of their idol and could not conceive that criticism was not necessarily iconoclasm. Some of them, as we gather, had abused Horace because he did not agree with their indiscriminating admiration. Moreover, at that epoch, a number of versifiers were reading their own productions whenever and wherever they could, — in the Forum or the public baths, or more especially in a certain Temple of the Muses, where prizes seem to have been awarded by a gentleman who went by the name of Tarpa. In this powerful polemic and compendium of the rules of style, Horace renounces for himself any such notoriety and asserts that he seeks the approval only of those whose opinion he values.

The preliminary lines are a subject for controversy. They are not found in a number of the manuscripts and are not mentioned by the scholiasts. Professor Lejay maintains that they are spurious and Professor Fiske, that they are genuine. " Who shall decide when doctors disagree? " Not I, in my ignorance, although I confess that I fail to discern those crudities of style which are apparent to some men of learning, and are not apparent to others.

The Cato mentioned is neither the Elder nor the Younger, but a well-known critic who had brought out an edition of Lucilius.

Talk Ten

Lucilius, how full of faults you are
I'll prove up to the hilt; and for my star
Witness, your own defender, Cato, cite
Who now designs your poems to rewrite;
And smoother he your ill-wrought verses can
Amend, because he is a better man,
And far more subtle than that other fellow
Whom as a boy wet ropes and straps would mellow,
Till he became a man who helped along
The bands of old against our squeamish throng,
Most learned of the knights grammarian;
And so let me return where I began.

Of course, I said some of Lucilius
Has the spring halt. What constant reader thus
An idiot, as to say he finds no blame?
And yet for the same poet on the same
Page you can see his merits rise and swell, 5
Because he salted down the city well.
For this, although I fitting tribute pay,
I cannot praise him every other way.
Laberius' farces then I'd have to call
Entirely lovely and poetical. 10
Therefore it's not enough for you to draw
Out of your audience a loud guffaw;
Though even here may virtue also lie.

Brevity is your need, winged thoughts that fly;
Nor, tangled up with verbiage, vex the ear;   15
Moreover in divers roles you must appear,
Sometimes you must be grave and often gay;
An orator's or poet's part you'll play.
And if you curb a too exuberant wit,
In lighter vein you'll make a heavier hit.   20
Better is ridicule and stronger too;
And, what vituperation cannot do,
Cuts to the heart of any great affair;
So you become the Old Comedians' heir;
Follow them if you want to get ahead,   25
Whom sweet Hermogenes has never read,
Nor that baboon who doesn't know a thing
Except for what of Calvus he may sing
Or else Catullus'. " But it's up to date
To mix up Greek and Latin; and it's great."   30
Does any highbrow really think it strange
Or difficult, which came in easy range
Even of Pitholeon the Rhodian
With lingo hybrid and barbarian?
" And yet his style where both the tongues combine,   35
Mellows, as when you mix the Chian wine
With the Falernian." If you write in verse,
Possibly yes. But what could be much worse
If you before the bar would plead the cause
Of poor Petillius, under Roman laws?   40
Have you forgotten father and fatherland,
While Pedius and Corvinus take their stand
To sweat their cause in Latin at the bar?
Would you mix words imported from afar
Like mongrel dialect Canusian?   45

I once to Greek in versifying ran
Though born this side the Adriatic sea.
Once after midnight 'twas forbidden me;
The God Quirinus came when dreams come true
And said: " 'Twould be far less insane for you   50
To carry corded fuel to the wood,
Than seek to swell that Grecian multitude."
So, while the turgid Alpine poet severs
The jugular of Memnon, or endeavors
To smear the River Rhine upon the head   55
With mud, I sport with fantasies instead.
Inside the Muses' Temple I'm not heard
Striving for Tarpa's ratifying word.
My Muse will never more return again
To charm the stage with popular refrain.   60
Fundanius, you above all living men
Delight with comedy the citizen;
How by the crafty tart and serving lad
Old money hog most properly was had.
With triple beat, the lyre of Pollio sings   65
The famed historic deeds of former kings;
And none so strong as Varius brings forth
A personage and deed of epic worth;
The country Muses never look askance
At dulcet Virgil's Attic elegance;   70
But though what I may write may better be
Than Gallic Varro and his company,
I'm not the peer of him who could invent
That style. Detraction I have never meant.
Nor vainly would endeavor to pull down   75
From off his head, his most illustrious crown;
And yet his verse is full of mud, I say;

And carries more that should be taken away
Than should be left. If you a scholar be,
Can you no frailties in great Homer see? 80
Lucilius himself, though most urbane,
Finds much to change in Accius' tragic strain
And laughs at Ennius' ungainly verse,
Yet calls his own no better, if not worse.
What stops us then, Lucilius' lines who read, 85
To ask if native talent or indeed
The dull, prosaic nature of his theme
Denied that fluency which we moderns deem
Poetry? With six-foot verses quite content,
On momentary inspiration bent 90
Two hundred he could write e'er food he munched,
The selfsame number after he had lunched.
For Tuscan Cassius, though his talents seem
More violent than the rapids of a stream,
His whole edition cast upon the fire, 95
Made up the fuel for his funeral pyre.
Urbane of wit Lucilius was, I say.
Moreover from his verse he filed away
More than the crowd of elder poets, more
Than any Roman who had gone before. 100
Much beauty, we'll admit, 'twere vain to seek
In a new form not extant in the Greek.
But if by fate born to a later age,
Much of his stuff he'd cut from every page
And smooth away what to diffuseness led. 105
In making verse he'd often scratch the head;
And often to the quick, he'd bite the nail,
When to a perfect verse he would prevail.
With right good reading if a page you'd grace

You'll often turn the pencil to erase. 110
Rub down your verse, nor labor for the loud
And vulgar admiration of the crowd.
Your readers should be few. Let scribbling fools
Desire their songs recited in grade schools.
Not I. "The knights' applause will do for me," 115
So said the spunky little Mistress Tree
Hissed by the hoodlums in the gallery.
Pantilius, the bedbug, shall he sting
Me, or Demetrius my withers ring
Talking against me when I am not present? 120
Or Fannius the moron prove unpleasant
Who cribs his dinners from Hermogenes
Tigellius? If my lucubrations please
Plotius and Varius and Maecenas too;
And Valgius and Virgil give them due 125
Praise; and Octavius one of the best,
Fuscus, each Viscus, also I attest
You in no fawning spirit, Pollio;
And you, Messalla, and your brother also
And Bibulus and Servius; so I can 130
Name Furnius, a very candid man;
And many others of my learned friends
Whom I pass over for my prudent ends.
I with my verses mainly try to please
The souls of good companions such as these; 135
With me I'd have them laugh; and if it be
Less than I hoped, it's just too bad for me.
Demetrius and Tigellius, get you gone;
Wail to the Woman's Clubs your monotone.
Go, lad, transcribe these lines and mind you look 140
Alive and add them to my little book.

HORACE TALKS

BOOK II

BOOK II

I · A Lawyer's Opinion

THIS snappy dialogue was composed about 30 B.C., while Trebatius was still alive. That veteran lawyer, friend of Cicero and partisan of Julius and Augustus, was recognized as an authority on Roman jurisprudence. He seems to have been acquainted with Maecenas, to have acted for him professionally, and last but not least, to have had a sense of humor.

It is possible that Horace had actually consulted Trebatius as to whether certain passages in the former satires were actionable; for the Roman laws of libel were complicated and severe, and Horace was a very careful man. However that may be, it seems to me extremely probable that Trebatius looked over this dialogue before it saw the light of day, and did not object to its publication. The Second Book of *Sermones* is much more sparing of personalities than the First; and this may be partly due to legal advice.

While in no wise contradicting his previous strictures on the style of Lucilius, Horace in this Talk pays him a magnificent tribute for character and genius. The friend of Maecenas seems anxious to do for the Imperium what the friend of Scipio had already done for the Republic. But Horace has distanced Lucilius in the race. Both the old satirist and the old jurisconsult owe most of their fame to his verses. In these they live and move and have their being.

Pope did Talk One into English and modernized it in the eighteenth century manner. He also paraphrased portions of it in his *Epistle to Dr. Arbuthnot*.

Talk One

HORACE: They're some to whom my satire sharply
    sounds,
Who say I strain my style beyond all bounds;
While others criticize what I compose
As nerveless, for a thousand lines like those
Could be turned out upon a single day.   5
Advise, Trebatius, what to do or say.
TREBATIUS: Keep still.
H.   You really mean I'm not to try
My hand at making any more?
T.   Aye, aye!
H. Damnation if it isn't for the best —
But sleep would never give me any rest!   10
T. Three times with oil you must rub down each limb
And then across the Tiber you must swim.
And if you can't sleep then, you will do right
To irrigate yourself with wine at night.
Or if for scribbling you have such desire   15
Tell about Caesar, our unconquered sire;
Your labors then will bring a great reward.
H. I only wish I could; but that's too hard
For my poor powers. Not everyone describes
Spear-bristling ranks, nor shattered Gallic tribes, 20
Nor wounded Parthian, falling from a steed.
T. Then write of Caesar himself. You can indeed,

A Lawyer's Opinion

Valiant and just, for all the world to know,
As sage Lucilius wrote of Scipio.
H. I'm ready for the hour this can be done; 25
But Flaccus' word without occasion
Would reach his listening ear not very quick.
Stroke the wrong way and you will get a kick!
T. Much wiser and much better that would be
Than flaying with your dreadful pleasantry 30
"The spender Nomentanus, and the clown
Pantolabus." Why everyone in town,
Himself unscathed, is for himself afraid
And hates the poet who the verses made,
Although that man you happen not to flout. 35
H. What can I do? Milon will hop about
When once hot wine has stroked him on the head
And banquet lamps a double lustre shed.
Castor the horses and the race tracks loves;
His twin from that same egg, the boxing gloves; 40
None of a thousand men shall ever live
Whom Fate does not a different hobby give.
Enclosing words in verse is my delight
According to the old Lucilian rite.
Better than you or I in aims and ends 45
The books he made were like familiar friends;
To them he told his secrets; he'd repair
To them for good or ill, nor turn elsewhere.
The life of this old poet stands out clear
As any votive tablet will appear. 50
I follow him, whate'er my stock may be,
Lucanian or Apulian ancestry.
The settlers of Venusia furrows trace
O'er the contiguous boundary of each place.

For both these races that same boundary held 55
When formerly the Sabines were expelled.
So runs the tale. Neither could hope to win
Through vacant land, invasion to begin
Of Rome; for equally these races are
Prone to run wild in violence of war. 60
But this shall be my sword which is my pen,
By my good will still sheathed for friendly men;
For why should I that brand attempt to draw,
Protected from vile robbers by the law?
I'm peaceful, but I brook no injury. 65
I cry out loud: " Better not pick on me! "
Who stirs me up, from him shall tears be wrung;
Notorious through the city he'll be sung!
Cervius, when angry, threatens with the law;
Canidia's poison gluts a foeman's maw, 70
That she has purchased from Albucius;
While mulcted you will be by Turius,
The judge, if you before his bar appear;
Each has a weapon which his foemen fear
So to prevail against them in the fight. 75
Thus potent Nature orders all aright,
As I deduce. With teeth a wolf is born;
A bullock tries to gore you with his horn;
Prompted by instinct bred within the bone,
Give Scaeva, for extravagance well known, 80
A mother whose days are long within the land;
No wrong is done her by his pious hand.
No wonder; ne'er a wolf kicks with his heels;
A bull in battle ne'er his teeth reveals.
Honey with hemlock tainted, one fine day 85
Shall carry the old dowager away.

A Lawyer's Opinion

No longer such examples will I bring.
If calm old age awaits, or the black wing
Of death may suddenly around me fly, —
Rich, poor, — in Rome, or if to exile I   90
May be ordained by Fate, my life shall be
In every color written down by me.
T. Beware! You won't live long, lad. I misdoubt
That some of your fine friends will freeze you out.
H. What! when of old Lucilius has dared, —   95
And to this end has poetry first prepared
For whoso strutted in a lion's skin,
To strip it off and show the ass within!
Did Laelius find anything to blame,
Or who from fallen Carthage earned his name, —   100
When Caelius Metellus fared the worse,
Or Lupus smothered in satiric verse?
Patricians and Plebeians both alike
With every word our satirist would strike
Impartially he sought the noblest ends,   105
And favored only Virtue and her friends.
When kindly Laelius and brave Scipio
Far from the madding crowd with him would go,
They and the poet simple amusement got
While boiled their cabbages inside the pot.   110
Though I may be in genius and in fame
Below Lucilius' undying name,
Envy, though loath, admits beyond debate,
I too have passed my days among the great.
If in soft flesh she tries to sink her teeth,   115
She'll bite against what's solid underneath.
Learned Trebatius, do you dissent?
T. There's nothing I can find for argument.

Only take care. Give ear to what I warn,
Lest sacred Law catches your ignorant scorn.   120
For as the brazen tablets all rehearse,
If one against his neighbor write bad verse
Those scurrile lines may actionable be
According both to law and equity.
H. Why, if the poem's bad, so may it be;   125
But if it's good, a better fate I see.
What if the verses gain great Caesar's praise?
What if a man the hue and cry should raise
Against a neighbor who deserves the shame,
Whereas the poet's record, none can blame?   130
T. The case will be laughed out of court. You'll be
Fully acquitted and you'll go scot-free.

BOOK II

II Plain Living

As with money in the First Talk of Book One, and as with women in the Second, Horace now preaches moderation in eating and drinking — plain living and high thinking — a regimen neither sordid nor extravagant. He pretends to note down the opinions of Ofellus, a farmer dispossessed by one of Caesar's soldiers, — a man whose self-reliance is one of the memories of his childhood. Personally I believe that he did know a man like that, who became for him an incarnation of old-fashioned rustic valor and virtue, all too rare in later times.

> " Damnosa quid non imminuit dies?
> Aetas parentum, peior avis, tulit
>   Nos nequiores, mox daturos
>   Progeniem vitiosiorem."

If the example of Ofellus could not stop that disastrous decline, nothing could, not even sumptuary laws.

It has been remarked that the maxims of Ofellus are an *omnium gatherum* from the Stoics, the Epicureans, the Cynics, Cicero and Lucilius; and that the excoriation of the millionaire who prefers ostentation to good works may be the result of conversations with Maecenas, and possibly with Augustus himself. But wherever these sayings came from, they are so arranged as to build up a character to whom

Horace does honor, and in doing so, does well. If such a man never existed, so much the better for Horace's creative genius, and so much the worse for the Imperium. But I believe that he did exist, and others like him, even while the damnable days were growing more damnable; for such men as these made possible " the grandeur that was Rome."

Pope has translated this talk with Georgian embroidery, but his translation lacks the tang of the original.

Talk Two

Learn how much character plain living wrought,
(Not my own words, but what Ofellus taught.
The farmer was illiterate, but full
Of homespun common sense. He was all wool
And a yard wide.) Good friends, we won't debate   5
Over a table garish with its plate;
Where all is senseless glamor, and the eye
Is duped with every mad effulgency.
By that false glare the dazzled mind is blent
To all the things that are more excellent.   10
Now, on an empty stomach, man to man
We'll talk, " Why so? " I'll tell you if I can.
By any judge for whom a price is paid
The truth is always very badly weighed.
If, following the hare, you're tuckered out,   15
Or by unbroken stallion jounced about;
Or if the Roman drill has made you weak,
Accustomed as you are to ape the Greek;
Or if you like to drive the day away
At games of ball where work is veiled as play;   20
Or if the discus beckons (seek you there
To hurl it through the acquiescent air); —
When good hard exercise has knocked you out,
What can you be fastidious about,
Empty and dry to kick at simple fare?   25

Would you alone to mead made up of rare
Honey from Mount Hymettus then incline
Diluted with the choice Falernian wine?
The butler's out; the fishes, safe at sea
In stormy depths refrigerated be.   30
Then will a yelping stomach find no fault
At getting some relief from bread and salt.
How do you think your appetites arise?
Not in rich viands the highest pleasure lies,
But in yourself. So by the sweat of exercise 35
Earn your *hors-d'œuvres*. For bloated gluttons pale
No help in oysters, trout, or foreign quail.
Yet hardly shall I ever disillusion
Your mind where Vanity has made confusion.
If you're at dinner where a peacock's served, 40
Your admiration never can be swerved
To realize a fowl does just as well
For tickling up the palate. Peacocks sell
For gold. Rare was the bird on which you fed —
Brave pageantry of painted tail outspread.   45
That's all beside the point, I may repeat.
Say, do you find his feathers good to eat
Which you esteem so highly? Do they look
So lustrous when they're sent in by the cook?
As for their meat, the peacock and the hen   50
Are just the same. Why will you rather then
Prefer the former, hoodwinked when you see
Their looks are different? So may it be.
But when you see a yawning pickerel
By what supernal instinct can you tell   55
Whether at Tiber's mouth, or in the course
'Twixt bridges twain, or at the Tuscan source,

'Twas caught? You relish well a three-pound mullet
In many slices that goes down your gullet.
You're dazzled by appearances, I see,   60
And crazy as a man may ever be.
What is the reason why you do not like
The large dimensions of the common pike?
Only because the pike's by nature wrought
Heavy and long; the mullet, light and short.   65
Only a stomach seldom hunger-torn
Holds ordinary nourishment in scorn.
" But I just love to see a great big fish
Laid out before me on a great big dish! "
Remarks a maw most worthy of rapacious   70
Harpies. But O, you southern winds, be gracious
And turn his tidbits rotten to the core.
Although fresh turbot and a fresh wild boar
Will stink in their perfection on the table
For overloaded stomachs, hardly able   75
To settle any food without a stir.
Radishes and dill pickles they prefer.
Nor is a poor man's diet even today
From royal banquets banished quite away,
Where eggs and black ripe olives hold their place.   80
Gallus the salesman served to his disgrace
A sturgeon at his board in days of old.
Did then the briny deep no turbots hold?
Safe was the turbot; safe in every nest
In former times, the stork could find a rest,   85
Until a would-be praetor set the fashion.
Why even roasted gulls would be a passion,
If someone made an edict one fine day
Which Roman youth would readily obey,

By Nature drawn to everything that's wrong. 90
Right here Ofellus' judgment comes out strong
That frugal eating must not sordid be.
What is the use a single vice to flee
When to its opposite, perverse, you turn?
Avidienus, who may richly earn 95
The name of hound that rightly to him stuck,
Eats five year olives and the fruit you pluck
From the wild cherry in the woodland bower,
And grudgingly pours wine unless it's sour.
When robed in spotless white, a birthday fete 100
Or wedding breakfast he may celebrate,
Or other holiday may be at hand,
His store of oil, whose smell you cannot stand,
He'll pour on cabbages, with his own hand,
From a great horn that weighs a couple of pounds, 105
And drop by drop the dressing goes the rounds.
But what he has in plenty and to spare,
Old vinegar he'll lavish everywhere;
For stinginess or vulgar loud display
Which of the two is more in Wisdom's way? 110
Here the wolf grabs you, runs the ancient saw,
And there the dog will grapple with his jaw.
A man alone may decent live and clean,
And ne'er offend by anything that's mean,
Who holds a middle ground both firm and stable 115
In neither manner to be miserable.
Not like old man Albucius he behaves,
Who for efficient service beats his slaves;
Nor Naevius, who facile is to please
And serves his guests with water tinged with grease, —
This too a major vice in minor things. 121

Plain Living

Now pray consider what plain living brings.
First comes good health. Do you not realize
The harm it does a man to gormandize
Day after day? Oh, then remember too,   125
How much plain living once agreed with you;
But just as soon as boiled and roast you mix,
Or thrush and shellfish, you'll be in a fix;
For what is sweet will turn itself to bile
When slow your stomach turns in tumult vile.   130
For all who rise from an elaborate meal
Do you not see what pallor they reveal?
Truly a body that's unwieldy grown
With yesterday's indulgence must weigh down
The soul. That godlike and ethereal birth   135
Is almost all cast down upon the earth.
But he who careful diet has preferred
Drops off to sleep before you say a word,
And lively on the morrow he'll uprise,
Ready for all prescribed activities.   140
A man to richer food might wend his way
When the recurrent year brings holiday,
Or if the body's weakness he'd assuage,
Or when the years advance to fond old age
And easier life. But how is it to be   145
With you, anticipating luxury
In prime of youth, while still the years press on,
And slow old age creeps near, and health is gone?
The men of old, who dwelt in days of yore,
Were loud in praises of a rancid boar,   150
Though not because they hadn't any nose;
But this was their opinion, I suppose.
Whenever a casual guest happens in late

From fish and gamy meat upon his plate
He'll get more comfort than the master host   155
Who greedily devours a fresher roast.
Full fain were I upon an early morn
Of Earth, amid such heroes to be born.
You can't be deaf to reputation, —
More sweet than song its music steals upon   160
The human ear. Big turbots on a plate
As large, will make a scandal quite as great —
And ruin you besides, — your uncle's ire,
Your neighbors, and your own frustrate desire, —
For when you want to hang, you cannot hope   165
To earn a cent to get a piece of rope.
" Oh is that so? " one answers. " Trausius
With talk may be excoriated thus;
But me, my interest a big income brings;
I'm rich enough to satisfy three kings."   170
Then why do you not find a better end
For circulating cash that you expend?
Why the deserving poor, with you so rich?
Why the old temples mouldering in the ditch?
Why, scoundrel, for your own dear fatherland   175
Not dole out something from a pile so grand?
For you alone shall business always be
Gilt-edged investment in prosperity?
Oh how ridiculous you'll look some day
To all the enemies who come your way!   180
Which of the two more safely may confide
In the uncertainties of time and tide, —
The man who has grown used in body and mind
To ostentation, or the man inclined
To be content with little luxury,   185

Plain Living

Who looks out for the future anxiously
And when at peace makes ready for the war?
You may believe how true these precepts are,
More readily when I tell you I have known
Ofellus long before I was half-grown.   190
And when he had his property intact
He never spent more cash for what he lacked
Than now he spends when Fortune has him downed.
You'll see him on his confiscated ground
Sturdily toiling with his flocks and sons,   195
A tenant now who was the owner once.
" I never gobbled rashly," he will say.
" 'Twas spinach and cured ham for every day;
In rainy weather, when I was not able
To work, a neighbor visiting my table   200
Would find no fancy fish that came from town
But kid or chicken; raisins and the brown
Nuts and split figs would ornament my board;
And afterwards a game we could afford;
We chose an umpire and we put away   205
The drink; who broke the rules must forfeit pay;
We drank to Ceres' sprouting corn divine;
From care the wrinkled brows were smoothed with wine.
Let ravening Fortune stir up strife and stress;
How much by this can She our lives depress?   210
Less stout and sleek do you or I appear,
My boys, since the new owner came in here?
Decrees of Nature never shall design
This plot of earth as either his or mine;
He drove us out; extravagance, in turn,   215
Or tangles of the law he does not learn,
Or certainly, at any rate, his heir

Surviving him, at last shall strip him bare.
This field is now under Umbrenus' name
That formerly under Ofellus came; 220
But truly 'tis the property of none —
Now used by me, now by another one.
And so live bravely; front with a brave breast
Strokes of ill luck that put you to the test.

BOOK II

III · STOIC HARANGUE

THIS tremendous diatribe purports to be a Stoic discourse as elucidated by one Stertinius (who is said by the scholiasts to have turned out two hundred volumes) and as reported by a certain Damasippus, a type of Greek adventurer that for years had infested the Metropolis. The *Sermo* lays down the doctrine that nearly all the world is insane, and endeavors to establish that thesis under five heads, namely, love of money, ambition, extravagance, love of women, and superstition. It elaborates a gross exaggeration by means of extreme examples. Its over-statements violate the very rules of sanity, of which their exponent and his disciple profess to be exemplars. The ridiculous Stoic is made even more ridiculous by the recital of a neophyte who, as Horace remarks in his final line, is crazier than the man he tries to enlighten. The *Sermo* is full of double-distilled humor. The more you read it, the more you get.

It has been noted that Damasippus, in quoting from his original, dilates for nearly half the *Sermo*, on money-making, and as he proceeds through the other four sections, becomes more and more sketchy. I do not think that this was merely on account of a defective memory, but because the newly converted Stoic was principally interested in getting rich quick. Of the other subjects, he only remembers salient examples. When he tells you how to get out of paying what you owe, he is very precise and definite. When he talks about superstition or the love of women, he is much more abrupt. His report of his master's discourse reveals his own inherent vulgarity.

But even so, his examples of extreme folly are memorably amusing. The inflated egoism of Agamemnon, the peculiar and spectacular career of Nomentanus who talks like a parlor pink, the freeman who prayed the gods to make him immortal, because it meant very little to them, these and half a hundred others taken from comedy and tragedy, both Greek and Latin, and from the ebullitions of numberless writers on philosophical subjects, are all profoundly comic. They serve to epitomize, in more ways than one, the dangers inherent in the transgression of the Golden Mean.

But the rant of Damasippus has its strong points. Some of the precepts, however misapplied, are based on a sane and solid philosophy. For example, his stricture on avarice and extravagance, the parallel vices of miser and spendthrift, comes, I believe, out of Aristotle. Later it was embodied in Roman Catholic theology and was illustrated by Dante. His overwhelming portrayal of these twin sins may be found in the Seventh Canto of the Inferno.

Talk Three

Damasippus: You write so seldom. Not four times a year
You search the rolls of parchment when you clear
Up final drafts; and what you now have writ
You niggle at and try recasting it;
Angry because to slumber and to wine   5
You show yourself too friendly and benign;
Whereas you never bring a poem out
That's worth its while even to talk about.
How will you end? Here to your rustic home,
To dodge the Saturnalia you have come.   10
Say something with some kind of dignity
That sounds like what you promised once to be.
Start up! There's nothing there. In vain you call
Down blame upon the pen or harmless wall,
For wrath of gods and poetasters born.   15
Yet once your visage threatened to adorn
Your pages with full many a splendid thing,
If only free from trouble you could sing
All snug and warm under your cottage roof.
How could it ever help in your behoof   20
To pack up Plato and Menander too,
Eupolis and Archilochus; for you
Such a fine company to bring up here?
And do you think when leisure now comes near,
And all your pristine virtue has gone by,   25

The envy of the crowd you'll pacify?
Poor dabbler! do you think you'll be exempt
From all their contumely and contempt?
Either abjure the wicked Siren Sloth,
Or quit your better life and be not loath.   30
HORACE: O Damasippus, for your counsel brave
May god or goddess grant you get a shave!
How come you ever knew me quite so well?
D. Ever since all my business went to Hell
By Janus' arch among the bulls and bears,   35
I muscle into other folk's affairs,
Jounced out of mine. Bronze bowls are on my beat,
Where sly old Sisyphus had washed his feet.
If crudely chiseled, or if cast too rough,
An expert's price I put upon the stuff —   40
A thousand bucks! I cleverly can buy
Up gardens and fine mansions. Who but I
Could make a profit; so that everyone
In crowded streets called me the favorite son
Of Mercury?
H.   You were sick. Of that I'm sure.   45
I often wondered how you found a cure.
D. Marvelously the new drives out the old,
As when a headache has you in its hold,
Or stitch in side, whose pain you can't appease —
They easily turn into heart's disease.   50
Or when the dopey patient turns about,
Puts up his fists, and knocks the doctor out.
H. Well, have it your own way; but make it clear
That nothing of the sort occurs round here.
D. Good sir, don't fool yourself. You're raving mad,   55
And any other fool is just as bad,

Stoic Harangue

If what Stertinius bellows has some truth.
I noted down his doctrines in good sooth.
From the Fabrician bridge I turned away,
A wiser man, and not so sad, that day 60
When I was broke and wished to hide my head
And throw myself down in the river bed.
He stood at my right hand. Said he: " Don't do
Anything that may discredit you.
The shame is false that gives you such a pain 65
You fear by madmen to be called insane.
What madness is I will inquire at first;
If you're the only one who so is cursed,
With not another word I'll waste my breath
To halt you on your valiant way to death. 70
Whom idle, evil folly and a mind
All ignorant of truth have stricken blind,
Chrysippus' porch and flock pronounce insane;
Save for a few with better balanced brain,
Great nations with their countless multitudes 75
And mighty kings this formula includes.
As in a forest wandering far and wide
Out of the beaten track on either side,
One to the left, one to the right, will make
In different ways the very same mistake. 80
Believe yourself insane, but know that he
Who may deride you will no wiser be;
To him has some one also tied a tail,
Which witlessly he drags along the trail.
There is one kind of gump who takes alarm 85
When nothing need be feared to do him harm.
Of fire or flood or rocks he will complain
That seem to block his way across the plain.

There is another and a different kind.
No wiser than the former as you'll find;　　　　90
Into the raging flood he'll plunge entire;
And run right through the middle of the fire.
Fond mother, loyal sister, all his kin,
Father and wife in vain may raise a din —
' Here's a big ditch and that's a rock! Look out! '　　95
He pays no more attention when they shout
Than drunken Fufius who took the part
Of sleeping Ilione with such art
He actually snored upon the stage!
And all in vain must Catienus rage;　　　　100
' Mother I call you,' would the ghost begin;
Ten thousand strong the audience joined in!
In such delirious madness I will show
How the whole crowd goes wandering to and fro.
When Damasippus bought old statues, he　　　　105
Was an example of insanity.
But Damasippus' creditor you find
Entirely to be in his right mind?
All well and good. Supposing I should say,
' Receive this cash you never can repay.'　　　　110
Would you be mad, accepting with good grace,
Or would you be more surely off your base
If all that pile of booty you should flout
That Mercury in person handed out?
In vain the creditor makes him scribble ten　　　　115
Drafts upon Nerius. Not enough? Why then
Throw in a hundred vouchers written by
Cicuta who well knows what knots to tie,
And bind him down as with a thousand chains;
But naughty Proteus still eludes your pains.　　　　120

Stoic Harangue

Hale him in court to answer for his debt —
Only the merry ha ha you will get!
Now boar, now bird, and now a stone he'll be;
And if he likes, he will become a tree.
If madness marks mistaken search for gain   125
And doing the contrary is good and sane,
Believe me, far more screwy is the head
Of a Perellius going in the red
By drawing up a bond in any way
Which you, his debtor, never can repay.   130
Smooth down your togas; listen, everyone
Whose cheeks grows pale with vile ambition,
Or who with lust of gold or luxury
Or with sad superstition fevered be,
Or many other ills of many a kind   135
That sorely may afflict a human mind;
Come nearer, while I show in order plain
How each and all of you have gone insane!
To all who hoard an avaricious store
We give the largest dose of hellebore.   140
Just why the whole caboodle should not go
Straight to Anticyra, I do not know.
Staberius to his heirs an order gave
To chisel what he owned upon his grave;
Or else for the arena when he died,   145
A hundred gladiators to provide;
To give a banquet served in such a state
As lavish Arrius would estimate;
And furnish so much grain for public cheer
As Africa could harvest in a year.   150
' Whether what I have willed is right or wrong,
I won't be lashed by any uncle's tongue;

So don't you try to put it over me.'
I think Staberius' prudence could foresee
That outcome. 'Why then all of his affairs   155
Did he arrange, so that he willed his heirs
To carve his patrimony on a stone?
What is the reason why he so has done?'
Long as he lived, he thought of poverty
As deep disgrace and dire monstrosity —   160
A thing he must avoid at any cost;
For if a single penny he had lost
He'd be no good upon the day he died.
That was his thought, and nothing else beside.
For he believed fair fame and honesty   165
And worthiness and common decency
And everything both human and divine,
The pulchritude of riches could outshine.
Heaping them up, he'd be in his own eyes
Famous and brave and just. 'Would he be wise?'   170
Why yes. He even then could be a king;
Or for that matter he'd be anything
He liked. For only virtue cash could raise;
And so he hoped for universal praise.
Now what is the similitude to seek   175
Between the man I mentioned and a Greek
Called Aristippus? Once the slaves he told
To throw away the burden of his gold
Whilst lumbering slow across the Libyan plain.
Which of the two would be the more insane?   180
You cannot with precision state your case
By setting opposites up face to face
And then their natures try to reconcile.
If one buys lutes and stacks them in a pile

Stoic Harangue

When nothing of much interest he can see 185
Either in music or in poetry,
Or if another, time and money lose
On knives and lasts, but cannot cobble shoes,
Or if another acquires avidly
The sails of ships but never trades at sea; 190
Everywhere would people rightly find
That such a man had gone out of his mind.
Is the discrepancy so very wide
From those who hoards of golden coin will hide
All ignorant of what their uses bring, 195
Afraid to meddle with a sacred thing?
If some one crouched beside a towering heap
Of corn, and with a club his watch would keep,
And dared not touch a single grain of wheat,
But bitter foliage instead would eat; 200
If full a thousand jars of Chian wine
And old Falernian — not much in fine,
Three hundred thousand say — if every jar
The owner saved, and drank sour vinegar;
Or if a man near eighty beds on straw, 205
While, stored away for moths and worms to gnaw,
A wealth of costly coverlids he's got
Inside his wardrobe, where they go to rot;
He'd seem insane to pitifully few,
Because what he has done, most men would do, 210
Plagued by the same disease in their affairs.
You god-forsaken gaffer, shall your heirs,
Either a son or even a freedman slave,
Drink down the property you try to save?
You think you'll be hard up? Why every day 215
How little extra money need you pay

And live so much the better when you spread
Oil on your cabbage or your scurvy head!
'My budget now is good enough for me.'
Why then do you resort to perjury?　　　　　　220
Why rob and plunder everywhere for gain?
And why do you suppose that you are sane?

By hurling rocks if you a crowd would smash
Or else the slaves for whom you paid out cash —
Why all the boys and girls would very soon　　225
Be shouting you were crazy as a loon.
But if perchance you finish off your wife
By strangulation, or your mother's life
By poison, will your head be quite intact?
'Why not? In Argos I did no such act　　　　　230
And never in the mad Orestian way
With iron sword did I a parent slay.'
Do you suppose Orestes went insane
The moment that his mother he had slain?
The wicked Furies rode him long, before　　　235
His keen-edged blade grew tepid in the gore
Of mother's jugular. Thenceforward he
Was held to be as mad as mad could be,
Yet nothing did that you can reprehend —
He never tried to violate his friend　　　　　　240
Pylades, nor Electra, with the sword,
Though cursing each with many a bitter word.
Her he called Fury; him with names as vile
As might be prompted by his livid bile.

Opimius was poor with all the gold　　　　　　245
And hoarded silver which he had in hold;

Stoic Harangue

On holidays he drank cheap Veian wine,
But otherwise his drink was not so fine.
From earthen scoop upon a working day
He only would imbibe the *vin du pais*.   250
One time a heavy stupor did him in,
And his glad heir in triumph could begin
To snoop around the strong box and the keys;
A loyal doctor, clever as you please,
Roused him up thus; he bade them place a stout   255
Table and pour the bags of money out
On it; and several people came to count
The coins and to determine their amount.
That got the old man up. The doctor said:
' Take care of what you own or you'll be bled.   260
Your greedy heir is ready now for plunder.'
' While I'm alive? ' ' Wake up, or else, by thunder,
You won't be. Do it now.' ' What do you want? '
' Your circulation's bad; your stomach can't
Function without the nourishment of food.   265
You're stalling. Come now, take a little good
Broth, if it's only this tisane of rice.
And do it now, right off.' ' What is the price? '
' Not much.' ' But just how much? ' ' Less than a dime.'
' Woe's me! What matters if I die from crime   270
Of theft and robbery, or because I'm ill? '
' Who then is sane? ' Who is not stupid? ' Still
What about misers? ' Stupid and insane.
' But one who's not a miser, is his brain
All right? ' Not much. ' Why, Stoic? ' I will make   275
It clear. A man has got no stomachache.
(Supposing Craterus speaks) Will he be so
Well he can get about? The answer's no.

His kidneys are affected, and his lung
Acutely. 'Here's a man will use his tongue   280
For truth, and to no pettiness incline.'
So let him give his kindly Lars a swine.
'But he's an upstart, throwing round his kale.'
Straight to Anticyra so let him sail;
What difference if you throw all you have got   285
Into a pit; or hoarding, use it not?

Servius Oppidius of Canusium
Had two estates, a very tidy sum
As reckoned in old days long since gone by.
He, dying, bequeathed two sons his property,   290
The story goes. He called them to his bed
And thus to both the boys the old man said:
'After I've seen you, Aulus, carry round,
Loose in your clothes what spillikins you found
And gamble them or give them all away —   295
And you, Tiberius, count them, day by day,
And hide them sombrely away in holes,
I judged your madness ran to different goals.
You follow Nomentanus in his wake;
You for a model would Cicuta take.   300
I urge you both that you most careful be
Not to increase, nor yet to make too free,
And with your patrimony play around,
Which father deems enough in Nature's bound;
And furthermore, lest glory tempt you both,   305
Herewith I bind you with a stringent oath;
If either seek an aedile's chair to fill
Or praetor's, he'll be cut out of my will —
And cursed besides. Why should you waste your means

Stoic Harangue

To lavish on the people peas and beans? 310
Why in the circus will you put on side
And scatter what you own, both far and wide?
Why should in bronze your crazy statue stand
Stripped of your father's money and his land?
The plaudits of the crowd Agrippa bore 315
Away. Would you like him come to the fore?
A furtive fox whoever can rely on
To ape the lordly grandeur of the lion? '

A burial for Ajax you deny,
O son of Atreus; will you tell me why? 320
' I am a king.'
    And I a common man;
No further will I question of your ban.
' I only have commanded what is right;
But if it seem injustice in your sight,
I will allow you without punishment 325
To tell me anything which you resent.'
Greatest of Kings! Now, by the gods I pray
You capture Troy and bring your fleet away.
Let me consult you how this thing may be;
And in return, will you respond to me? 330
' Consult.'
    Why is great Ajax left to rot
Who second only to Achilles got
Renown; so many combats has he braved,
So often your Achaeans has he saved.
Now Priam and his people will rejoice 335
That Ajax lies unburied by your choice;
When by his deeds the youthful progeny
Of Troy far from their home unburied lie.

' A thousand sheep to Death the madman gave
Crying he had abolished with his glaive   340
Renowned Ulysses, Menelaus, me —
Instead of these, in his mad butchery.'
When you to Aulis in a heifer's stead
Brought your sweet child and sprinkled on her head
Before the altar, salt and sacred meal,   345
Was there no madness in your soul to heal?
And what did Ajax more insanely do
When he drew sword upon the flock, than you?
From killing wife and child he would abstain.
His maledictions may have seemed insane   350
On Atreus' sons, but never did his arm
To Teucer or Ulysses' self do harm.
' 'Tis true my ships I'd rescue when they wore
Too long at anchor on an adverse shore.
I would conciliate of my own free will   355
The gods with blood.'
     You are a maniac still.
The blood was yours.
     ' Mine, but no maniac I.'
So we continue with our homily.
Whoever holds a concept that's untrue
And seethes with turmoil which to crime is due, 360
Is held to be unsettled in his mind.
It makes no difference if he err from blind
Folly, or be by anger led astray;
So Ajax, when the harmless lambs he'd slay,
Acts like a lunatic. When you begin   365
Deliberately to commit a sin
For empty honors, can you be quite sure
Of arrogance your mind and heart are pure?

Stoic Harangue

Suppose a female lamb of snow-white sheen
One loved to carry in a palanquin — 370
As to a daughter, furnished raiment rare,
Money, and maids, and called it Goldenhair
Or Tiny, and a husband tried to get,
A nobleman to wed the little pet,
A praetor's warrant will his rights restrain. 375
His custody devolves upon his sane
Relations. What if one his daughter gave,
Like a dumb lamb, to sacrificial glaive.
Will he be sound of mind? Ah! say not so.
When crime and folly hand in hand will go, 380
They reach the acme of insanity;
A criminal and maniac is he;
Glitter of vitreous fame will get him under
And bloodthirsty Bellona round him thunder.

Come now with me, and to the case advance 385
Of Nomentanus and extravagance;
We'll prove that any waster is a fool
And madman, also, under Reason's rule.
He came into a fortune, so I'm told,
More than a million dollars' worth of gold; 390
He issued then an ordinance, for all
Who fish or fruit were selling in a stall,
The poultry man and the perfumer too —
In short, from Tuscan Street, the whole damned crew.
The clowns and sausage-maker he'd arouse 395
And from Velabrum the whole slaughter house.
He told them at his home they were allowed
To come. What then? They came in a big crowd.
A pimp spoke up for them. 'What mine may be,

And all these others' household property, 400
Credit as yours. Go look for it today,
Or else tomorrow.' Listen to the way
This nice young man for answer would propose:
'You, in big boots, sleep in Lucanian snows
That I on a wild boar may dine at ease. 405
You sweep for fish over the wintry seas;
I'm lazy. All this gold is not my due.
Then take it. Here's a hundred grand for you —
And you. Three times that sum for such a one
Because his wife is always on the run, 410
If called up in the middle of the night.
And so he abrogates a husband's right.'

Aesopus' son took from Metella's ear
A pearl which at ten thousand was not dear,
In vinegar dissolved it to a pulp — 415
And so drank down ten thousand at a gulp.
Is he less sane who'd throw a gem so pure
Into a rapid river or the sewer?
Of Quintus Arrius the progeny,
A pair of brothers in nobility, 420
In folly and crime equally ill-behaved,
And twins indeed in love of what's depraved,
Would spend the sum such lavishness entails
To make their breakfast upon nightingales.
Where do they go? With chalk or charcoal mark? 425
Sane in the white or crazy in the dark?

To build toy houses or to hitch up mice
To a toy cart, or play at the device
Of odd or even, or ride on a long stick —

Stoic Harangue

A bearded man who really gets a kick 430
Out of such stuff is crazy in the head.
And may it not be reasonably said,
If you should fall in love and weep and wail
For any girl whose beauty is for sale,
More childish you'd not seem in Reason's eyes 435
When you were three years old and made mud pies?
I ask if you will do what Polemon
Did when he underwent conversion.
The symptoms of disease he put away,
His muffler, necklace, bracelets, so they say; 440
And from his neck he pulled off stealthily
The wreaths that he had worn in revelry;
Carried away by what the master said,
Before he'd taken wine or broken bread.
You hand out apples to a sulky child 445
And he's not having them. If thus beguiled:
'Take them, you little tyke,' he shakes his head;
Don't give, and he will beg for them instead.
And is the lover different who will pour
Out his complaint when he is shown the door? 450
Shall he go back or not, when he's been slighted,
Still yearning to return, though uninvited?
So with himself he still is at debate
And still he sticks around the hateful gate —
'When at long last she calls me, shall I go? 455
Or rather shall I finish up my woe?
She shuts me out! She'll call me to her doors!
Shall I go back? No! not if she implores.'
How infinitely wiser is the slave:
'Master, here is a thing which does not have 460
Anything like reason or a plan.

It is intractable for any man
A reasonable method to devise.
In any love there alternately lies
Evil. First war, then peace will come once more.   465
A stormwind rises only to blow o'er;
Blind chance will guide its advent and its flight;
No certain method ever sets it right;
Such permutations you'll no more explain
Than reasonably plan to go insane.'   470
When, snapping a Picenian apple seed
You hit the ceiling and are glad indeed
In the belief your love will reach its goal,
Are you the master of your mind and soul?
Or when your aged palate does not balk   475
At lisping out a line of baby talk,
How are you saner than a little boy
Who models funny houses for a toy?
Add blood to folly; stir the lover's flame
As with a sword. One Marius I could name   480
Who cut his sweetheart Hellas down of late
And frantically rushed to his own fate;
You might acquit that man of mental stress
And yet condemn him for his wickedness;
And in the many changes Custom rings   485
Label with synonyms the selfsame things.

A freedman once there was, an aged man
Who, fasting early in the morning, ran
With well-washed hands to pray the gods divine
At each street corner where there stood a shrine.   490
'It's only me. It's not so much,' he'd pray.
'I beg of you to steal my death away.

Stoic Harangue

That's easy for the gods.' Such was his prayer.
His eyes and ears a buyer'd find all there.
His mind a seller could not guarantee;   495
No master would insure his sanity,
Unless he liked a lawsuit on his hands.
This crowd, according to Chrysippus, stands
Right in with Looney's growing family —
As when a mother's little son must lie   500
Abed five months, malaria plagued him so;
Thus up to Jupiter her prayer would go:
' Great woes you give to man, and take away.
May chill malaria leave my boy, I pray,
And on your festal day, with dawn at hand,   505
All naked in the Tiber shall he stand! '
If luck or if the doctor should upraise
The boy and lift him out of danger's ways,
She'll plant him right upon the freezing shore
And chills and fever she'll bring back once more.   510
Thus she will tuck him underneath the sod.
What is her madness but the fear of god? "

So friend Stertinius armed me against fate;
Of seven sages he is number eight.
If I'm called mad, myself I'll now defend,   515
And give 'em back as good as they can send.
They'll know whose faults are dangling down behind
And, glancing back, a bagful they shall find.
H. Now that your failure, Stoic, has blown o'er,
May all your holdings liquidate for more   520
Than you have lost. So for insanity,
Tell me about my special malady.
For though my follies number more than one,

Myself I seem to be possessed of none.
D. What! when Agave bore in hands defiled 525
The severed head of her unlucky child,
Did she herself a raging maniac deem?
H. Folly I will confess (for it would seem
That I must yield to truth) and I'm insane.
Nevertheless I beg you will make plain 530
For me exactly what you think you find
As an affliction for a morbid mind.
D. Then first get this. You build. You try to ape
A man who's really great; whereas your shape
Is slight and squat and never will be more; 535
You only are a little two by four.
You laugh at the small Turbo heartily
When in his gladiatorial armor he
Must strut about and make a great big fuss.
Which of the two is more ridiculous? 540
Whatever Maecenas does, you want to do.
Can that be quite appropriate for you,
So different, so much punier, than he?
A match for him you cannot hope to be.
When mother frog was absent from her roof 545
A bull-calf crushed her brood beneath its hoof;
One got away and told her how a great
Monster the family wiped out of late.
She asked how big he was. "So great," quoth she,
"As that?" and up she swelled. "Not half," quoth he.
"As great as that?" she swelled out more and more. 551
"You cannot equal him. You'll burst before."
This image does not miss you by a hair.
Then add your poems. Pour oil upon the flare.
If anyone is sane who writes in verse 555

Stoic Harangue

You're surely sane your poetry to rehearse.
Your awful temper bursting every bond —
H. Mind your own business.
D.   And you live beyond
Your income.
H.   Damasippus, hush your noise!
D. You're crazy for the girls and for the boys,   560
A thousand each. You never will have done.
H. O greater madman, spare the lesser one.

BOOK II

IV De Rerum Natura

If Talk Three is a parody of the Stoic doctrines, Talk Four is a travesty of the Epicurean. We are told that the precepts about to be promulgated will vanquish Pythagoras, Plato and Aristotle. We find that they consist of a well-chosen *menu* of homegrown products, with recipes for a laxative and a settler for the stomach, together with a recommendation for cleanliness in service — details almost all of which would be familiar to any Roman matron who was on pleasure bent but had a frugal mind. Finally we have a highflown encomium on the Great Unknown who originally divulged the doctrines — an encomium based upon a stately passage of Lucretius. I fancy that the guests at some forgotten dinner party had a hearty laugh when they heard this Talk for the first time, and that it soon became a famous example of humorous anticlimax.

In Talk Three and Talk Four, the characters of the disciples are antithetical. Damasippus the Stoic, is aggressive, loud-mouthed, and vulgar; Catius the Epicurean, is bland, serious, and rather highbrow. But both are fatuous enthusiasts — the former with his wildeyed eagerness to make a convert to absurdity, the latter with the calm superiority of an initiate into the mysteries *De Rerum Natura*. Both transgress the Golden Mean — Damasippus by exaggeration and Catius by treating the obvious as a higher truth.

Talk Four was probably composed after the publication of Book One, i.e., between 35 and 30 B.C. There are many Greek and Lucilian sources.

Talk Four

HORACE: Whence come you, Catius, where do you go?
CATIUS: There is no time for me; for I am so
Anxious to note new doctrines, such as quite
Vanquish Pythagoras and erudite
Plato and him accused by Anytus.   5
H. I do confess my fault to quiz you thus
At such an inauspicious time. I pray
You pardon me, good friend. Whatever may
Escape you now, you'll presently recall.
Whether by art or nature this befall,   10
Your memory astounds in either case.
C. The whole discourse I'd carefully retrace;
A subtle matter must with subtlety
Be rendered into phraseology.
H. What's the man's name, before you tell the rest? 15
Is he a Roman or an alien guest?
C. From memory the doctrines I'll declaim.
As for the man, I would conceal his name.

Eggs long and lank, you'll preferably serve
For these a better flavor will preserve;   20
And larger are their whites, as doth appear,
Than those that close approximate a sphere;
And all their yolks are firm and masculine.
Cabbages from dry fields are far more fine

And sweet than those in suburb garden grown.   25
There's nothing of a more inspid tone
Than produce raised in irrigated land.
Now if a sudden guest should come to hand
At evening, and the fresh-killed fowl you fear
Tough to the tongue, will make him sorry cheer,   30
If you are wise, you'll practice what I urge;
While still alive, that chicken you'll submerge
In water mingled with Falernian wine —
And tender it will be, what time you dine.
And he will pass a summer healthily   35
Who ends his lunch with the black mulberry,
Plucked from the tree before the sun grows hot.
Aufidius all wrong a mixture got,
Honey and Falernian of a stalwart strain.
Strong drink will not befit the empty vein —   40
You'll wash your stomach better with mild mead;
And if the costive guts grow hard indeed,
Mussels and common shellfish will go through
The obstacle; and the dwarf sorrel too,
But not without White Coan wine as well.   45
All shellfish will distend within the shell
Under the crescent moon. But every sea
Yields not their excellencies equally.
Big bivalves dwelling in the Lucrine lake
Give better taste than Baian mussels take.   50
Circeian oysters hold the rest in scorn;
Sea urchins at Misenum are well-born,
And soft Tarentum on another coast
Of yawning scallops over all may boast.
But none should plume himself as epicure   55
Who knows not subtle flavors and their lure.

'Tis not enough to clear a high-priced stall
Of fish, if you be ignorant withal
Which served with sauce will give a keener zest;
Which better broiled, whereby the jaded guest   60
Will rise up on his elbow once again.
Acorn-fed boars from Umbrian hill or plain
That bend the platter down, to those appeal
Who fain would shun a flat and tasteless meal;
But the Laurentian boar is poor indeed   65
Waxed fat upon the sedge grass and the reed.
The vineyard will not always goats supply
That you can eat. If you'd act sapiently
Sever the shoulders of a pregnant hare.
For birds and fish, what qualities they bear   70
And what should be their age, was never known
By any palate, previous to my own.
Some genius candy would alone invent.
On one thing only be you not content
To concentrate; as though you would confine   75
Yourself to the avoidance of bad wine,
And never mind about the course of fish,
What sort of olive oil should douse the dish.
Under clear skies, set out the Massic wine —
The air of night its rawness will refine;   80
Nerve-wracking odors will not then remain.
With linen you will spoil it if you strain,
For thus it loses most of its bouquet.
For any connoisseur who knows the way,
Falernian lees be with Surrentine blent.   85
Be careful to scrape up the sediment,
Drop in its depths an egg of turtle dove;
The yolk all alien matter will remove.

De Rerum Natura

A man who's taken more than he can stand,
Revive with shrimps and snails from Afric's strand.
If salad with sour stomach you combine
The lettuce leaves will float upon the wine.
For prickly stimulation, he should cram
Rather with sausage or a slice of ham.
He'd even rather have what comes to hand
Sizzling and steaming from a hot dog stand.
'Tis worthy your attention thoroughly
To study compound sauce. Plain sauces be
Composed of oil of olive fresh and sweet,
With heavy wine commingling as is meet,
And brine identical with what will come
From stinking kegs out of Byzantium.
After you stir up well with herbs chopped fine
Sprinkle Corycian saffron on the brine,
Then boil and let it stand; as for the rest,
Add juices from Venafran olive pressed.
Tiburtine apples neath Picenian go
For succulence — but make a braver show.
Venuculan grapes are best in jars preserved;
The Alban, dried in smoke, are rightlier served.
I first of all upon the bill of fare
Put these with apples mixed; and caviare
I was the first to serve with dregs of wine.
White pepper and black salt both sprinkled fine
On separate saucers, I was first to find.
Now an enormity I'll call to mind —
To spend three hundred for a catch of fish
And then to squeeze them in a narrow dish;
Or if a slave passes a drinking cup
With greasy dripping hands, who's gobbled up

A fragment stolen from his master's plate,
It turns the stomach and may nauseate;
Or if in wine bowl, cast in days of old,
There still adheres a thick and horrid mould.
How small the price of napkins, sawdust, brooms!   125
Neglected how immense the scandal looms,
With dirty brush to swab mosaic floor
Or Tyrian tapestry to cover o'er
With unwashed cloth; mere cleanliness to spare.
Forgetful of its little cost and care,   130
How much more reprehensible for you
Such negligence, than to omit what's due
To large expenditure of ornament
Upon the tables of the opulent.
H. By friendship, learned Catius, I pray,   135
And by the gods, remember on that day
When to his lectures you once more repair,
And for the future, take me with you there;
For though from memory you can impart
All you have heard, and grave it on my heart,   140
You never may the loftiest pleasure bring
By mere report of this most marvelous thing!
For surely you were blessed beyond the norm
To look upon his countenance and form;
But afterwards you hardly realize   145
What such a sight must mean to other eyes.
Within me now there is no little care
To those sequestered fountains to repair
And all the doctrines I would quaff with zest —
So may I live my life among the blest.   150

BOOK II

V · How to Get Rich Quick

IN TALK FIVE, Horace gives a stinging description of the manoeuvres of a particularly lowdown individual, the fortune hunter who toadies for a legacy. These gentry seem to have been extremely common in Ancient Rome. Is the species altogether extinct today?

The setting is Homeric, and frequently the style. The dialogue is an irreverent continuation of the interview between Odysseus and Tiresias in the Νεκυία. It begins where Tiresias leaves off, with the famous prophecy that Odysseus will return in evil plight, in another man's ship, and after his companions have all been destroyed. The Horatian Ulysses, with an eye to the main chance, asks the shade of the Theban seer how he can make some money, and Tiresias proceeds to tell him how it can be done at Rome with its law courts and its wealthy but unvenerable old men and their satellites. The advice of Tiresias might be called "realistic," if not worse. This rather ignominious figure of a comic Ulysses came to Rome from Alexandria.

The lines about the policeman warmed over, the clerk and the gaping crow — apparently a queer combination of the tragedy of Medea with a fable from Aesop — have baffled generations of interpreters as they evidently baffled Ulysses. This oracular utterance Horace has not explained. But it seems to show, together with what immediately follows, that he had the same opinion of oracles as of miracles and witchcraft.

Furius Bibaculus, who has already been mentioned in the Tenth Talk of Book One, was a contemporary of Calvus and Catullus, one of the galaxy of "modern poets" whom Cicero did not approve of. He is said to have aggrandized his paunch with food and drink. The lines which Horace quotes have all the earmarks of an aspiring modernity. The value of the result has been given a lasting notoriety by the genius of Horace. It seems to me that we need a Horace today to label balderdash. Commentators are at variance as to what "dumb effigies" were "split." But there is a general consensus of opinion that the epithet in question is peculiarly adapted to the lines themselves.

Talk Five was probably written in the autumn of 31 B.C. after the battle of Actium.

Talk Five

ULYSSES: I pray, Tiresias, answer this beside
What you already told me would betide;
Tell me the arts and methods to restore
My property, that long has gone before.
Why laugh?
TIRESIAS: It's not enough for you to learn,   5
O man of wiles, some day you will return
To Ithaca, and there you will espy
Your household gods?
U.   You never told a lie
To anyone; and my return you see
Naked and penniless; thus the prophecy.   10
Cellar nor herd the suitors left intact.
Valor and birth, unless with money backed
Are cheap as seaweed.
T.   What you vaguely said,
Setting aside, 'tis poverty you dread.
Accept the methods, reasoned fair and plain,   15
How you'll be able to grow rich again.
Now if a thrush, or anything as nice
Be yours, its wings must bear it in a trice
Where great wealth gleams, by an old man possessed;
Sweet apples, or whatever else is best   20
To raise on well-tilled farm, with honors rare,
Before the Lar, let taste the millionaire.
No household god is worshipful as he.

However great a perjurer he may be,
An upstart whom a brother's blood doth lave, 25
Or else a runagate and once a slave,
You'll walk beside him in the sight of all
If asked, and not decline to give the wall.
U. What now? Must I a dirty Dama shield
From mud? It was not thus on Trojan field 30
I played my part, when I with better men
In combat strove.
T.   You'll be a pauper then.
U. Strong soul, I do commend thee suffer scorn
For greater ills in former days I've borne.
Augur, say on! How in a little while 35
I might dig up some cash and make my pile.
T. I've told you and I'm telling you in fine.
For old men's wills, throw out a crafty line.
If one or other may be fighting shy,
And nibbles at the hook and then darts by — 40
Don't give up hope and cast aside your art,
As though you had been hoodwinked at the start.
A case may be contested any day;
Inside the Forum, it might come your way.
It may be big or little, but if he 45
Who is the plaintiff, has no progeny,
And he is rich and scoundrelly to boot,
And he has brought a most outrageous suit
Against a better man, with better cause,
Defend the rascal under Roman laws. 50
Reject the other party to the strife;
He has a son at Rome and fertile wife.
" Quintus " or " Publius " say; for it appears
First names fall gratefully on tender ears.

How to Get Rich Quick

"Your inborn worth has made of me a friend. 55
Law tricks I know, and cases can defend.
I'd sooner someone gouged out both my eyes,
Than anyone your credit should despise,
Or of a nutshell you should pillaged be;
I'll take good care of you; so count on me. 60
You'll not lose anything; and when I'm done,
You shall not be a joke for anyone."
Tell him to take it easy and go home;
And you yourself his advocate become.
Press on! hang on! "Whether the Dog-star red 65
Split the dumb effigies," or Furius fed
Up with fat tripe, "spew wintry Alps with spray
Of hoary snow." — A bystander will say
Nudging the next one, "Did you ever see
So patient, deft, and keen a man as he?" 70
So several tunnies may swim up; and so
They swell your fishponds full to overflow.
And furthermore, if for resplendent wealth
A son's picked up, who may enjoy poor health —
And you don't want to be discovered for 75
A parasite to some old bachelor,
Wind round the father slowly, and, with care,
Your service may inscribe you second heir.
And if, perchance, the boy to Orcus be
Borne down, you'll step into the vacancy; 80
Such dice will very rarely fall untrue.
If someone hands his testament to you,
Refuse to read it and remember right
Sternly to push the tablet from your sight;
But cling with sidelong glance to this design, 85
On the first page to glimpse the second line.

And quickly gather if you're mentioned there
Alone, or else with many as co-heir.
Often a cop, boiled down and changing so
Into a clerk, may cheat the gawking crow.   90
To Nasica, who hunted easy money,
Coranus gave the prize for looking funny.
U. Have you gone mad, or would you sane, procure
To flout me with your oracles obscure?
T. Son of Laertes, all I say is what   95
Will either come to pass, or it will not.
For great Apollo hath bestowed on me
The divination and the prophecy.
U. But none the less, what mean the words you say?
And this, your legend, tell it if you may.   100
T. In future days, when over land and sea,
Feared of the Parthians, a youth shall be
Great, and from high Aeneas trace his birth;
Nasica's daughter, tall and wide of girth,
Unto the brave Coranus shall be wed.   105
Nasica'll owe him money and will dread
To pay it back. The son-in-law will so
Manage that to the father-in-law he'll show
His will and beg the other to peruse.
Full many a time will Nasica refuse;   110
But shall at last consent and silently
Read it, and find there's nothing that will be
Bequeathed to him or his except a tear.
But these aside, this law I lay down clear;
Suppose a freedman and a crafty dame   115
Manage a silly old man. Approach the same
As their ally; speak well of them, and when
You're absent, they'll speak well of you again.

How to Get Rich Quick

And that will help; but better far instead
Strike with your shafts directly at the head.   120
If he writes crazy doggerel, say it's great;
Or if he loves the ladies, do not wait
Till asked; but rather more obliging be —
To your superior, hand Penelope!
U. Is that your thought? Can she be led astray   125
So pure, so chaste, whom from the righteous way
The suitors were all powerless to seduce?
T. That gang was too hard up. They had no use
For scattering largess. Venus did not mean
Nearly as much to them as your cuisine.   130
Therefore Penelope is chaste and true.
As soon as she's in partnership with you,
To taste a little gain from some old man,
She'll be a regular hound who never can
Be shooed away from greasy undressed hide.   135
Now I will tell you something else beside.
In Thebes it happened once when I was old;
Of an old harridan the tale is told.
According to her will when she was dead
Thus her remains should be deposited.   140
When she was rubbed down thick with oil, her heir
On naked shoulders must her body bear
So that in death perhaps she could contrive
To give him once the slip; for when alive
He stuck right down on her, as I suppose.   145
Take care of your approach, be not of those
Who shirk their offices, nor backward bend
With overzeal. The garrulous offend
The aged who are captious and morose.
And on the other hand, be not of those   150

Who never talk. Comedian Davus be;
Stand with your head bowed low, obsequiously,
Much like a man who fears what might befall;
And hang around him at his beck and call.
If the breeze freshens, warn him Prudence said   155
To wrap up well his dear beloved head.
Straight through a crowd, you'll shoulder in your way
To fish him out; and if he talks all day —
At every foolish word, prick up your ear;
And if unmannerly, he wants to hear   160
His praises sung, follow him up with praise,
Until he shall to heaven his hands upraise
And shout " enough! " Blow up the windbag well,
And with your bombast make him puff and swell.
When free from that long servitude and care,   165
Look sharp to hear: " Ulysses is an heir
To a full quarter of my worldly store."
" Is Dama, the old comrade, now no more?
Where shall I find another such as he,
So noble and so loyal unto me? "   170
If you can manage it, squeeze out a tear
Of hidden joy your countenance to clear;
If in your jurisdiction it may come,
You shall not skimp when you erect his tomb;
And so the neighborhood will one and all   175
Exalt the fine and costly funeral.
If a co-heir who is an older man
Has a bad cough, you'll tell him how he can
Buy in some land or house that may belong
With your own share and have it for a song.   180
But Proserpine the powerful draws me to
Her realm once more. Long life and luck to you.

BOOK II

VI · "Of the Mean and Sure Estate"

This is a page from the daily life of Horace. It was probably written during the winter of 31–30 B.C. when he was in full enjoyment of the Sabine Farm. Octavian, who was campaigning against the Parthians, had left Maecenas in charge of affairs at Rome. Horace had been the friend of Maecenas for nearly seven years; and had become particularly important in the eyes of the multitude, not because of his poems, but because of his friendship. So he tells us how he was pestered by acquaintances — pestered in the Forum and at the entrance of Maecenas' gardens on the Esquiline — how people thought he must know state secrets, whereas most of the remarks that Maecenas addressed to him were discreetly banal — how he yearned for a good rest in the country where people talked about something worthwhile, where he could have the bean on his table, the transmogrified relative of Pythagoras (Horace here and elsewhere gently prods the doctrine of metempsychosis) and how he could listen to the fable of the country mouse and the city mouse, which ever since has set the pace for mice and men.

That fable is one of the major ornaments of literature. It originated with Aesop, but was changed by the alchemy of Horace's genius into something rich and strange. It has haunted the vision of poets for hundreds of years. It was charmingly paraphrased by André Chénier shortly before the French Revolution. In England in 1687, Prior and Montagu dilated upon it in a parody on Dryden. Together with the rest of the satire, Pope and Swift between them revamped it for Georgian taste as Cowley had already refurbished it for the garish court of old Rowley.

> "Where thousand beauteous shes about you move
> And by high fare are pliant made to love."

But that is by no means the first appearance in England. Away back in 1570, Sir Thomas Wyatt composed three satires at his country seat in Kent. The first of them, entitled " Of the Mean and Sure Estate " commences with a story of the " fieldish mouse " and her " townish sister," which is a variation of the Latin fable.

One could write a huge volume on Horatian echoes in English poetry. I will merely take Wyatt's three satires as an example. They are saturated with Horace from start to finish. Like many others, Wyatt finds that stray passages from his favorite can be inserted almost anywhere. So in the " Courtier's Life " you hear an echo of the lines in Talk Three, Book One, where Horace recommends that defects be euphemized. In "How to Use the Court and Himself " you hear an echo from Talk One where Horace speaks of the restlessness of the money-chaser; and further along we have an echo from Tiresias where Wyatt's correspondent is ironically advised to dance attendance on rich old age and hand over his " cousin, sister, and daughter " as Ulysses was advised to hand over Penelope to his superior. One could pile up other instances from other poets and become very tedious. I think I have said enough to prove my point, that Horace has permeated English literature ever since the reign of Henry the Eighth.

Talk Six

This was among my prayers, a moderate plot
Of ground — not near so large as what I've got —
A garden, too; and near my roof, a source
Of water running freshly on its course;
And over these a bit of woods might be;   5
Better by far the gods have done for me.
'Tis well; O Maia's son, no more I'll pray
Except you make this gift my own alway.
If I have never by bad business
Enlarged my store, nor yet will make it less   10
By folly or neglect; if on my knees
I never made such stupid prayers as these:
" Oh! If that neighbor's corner came to me
That spoils my little farmstead's symmetry!
Oh! If my luck could show in my own ground   15
Just such a pot of money as was found
Once by a hired man who with his yield
Of treasure bought that land and plowed that field!
Such coin a friendly Hercules had sent."
With what I have I'm happy and content.   20
Fat cattle are my prayer to you instead,
Everything fat except the owner's head.
Be with me now as you have been of yore;
My steadfast guide and guardian evermore,
When as remote from town up here I dwell   25
Among the mountains in my citadel.
What first can I illustrate by the use

Of satires and of my pedestrian Muse?
Here fell Ambition cannot do me harm,
Nor leaden Auster here can raise alarm, 30
Nor dreary Autumn with his guerdon come
For Libitina, goddess of the tomb.
O Father of the Morn, or if you'd rather
Lend me an ear as Janus than as father;
Whence, so it pleased the gods, the race of man 35
The work and labor of their life began,
Be thou the head and front of all my song.
If I'm at Rome, you make me hurry along
When I go surety for another's bond.
" Hi! never let another man respond 40
For Duty's call before you. Up and go! "
If Earth is blasted when the north winds blow
Or if the winter Solstice drags the day
In narrow circles on its snow-clad way
I start out just the same; and when I've lost 45
My cash in clearly worded legal cost,
I have to jostle through the crowd and goad
To injury the loiterers on my road.
" What do you think you're doing, you idiot?
What do you mean? Why do you think you've got 50
To run down everything that's on your way? "
Curses the irate scoundrel brought to bay;
" You only have Maecenas on your mind,
And back to him you run as you were blind."
That's sweet as honey and I tell no lie. 55
To the black Esquiline as soon as I
Have come, around me jump a hundred cares
And all of them are other men's affairs.
Right through my head they go, and all around

"Of the Mean and Sure Estate"

On every side of me they leap and bound. 60
"Roscius implores you not to come too late
To meet him at the Puteal at eight
Tomorrow." "Quintus, for the clerks today
There's a big deal that's getting under way.
Remember to come in. It's something new. 65
And have Maecenas seal these vouchers too."
"I'll try," you say. Says he insistent still:
"You sure can fix it, if you only will."
The seventh year has almost run its date,
And very nearly reaches Number Eight, 70
During which time Maecenas condescends
To have me in the circle of his friends;
So far as in his carriage when he'll take
Me for a journey he desires to make.
These are the little gems that he sees fit 75
To give me when he talks: "What time is it?"
Or "Is the Thracian bantam on a par
With Syrus?" or "These frosty mornings are
Liable to bite you, if you don't watch out."
And other things one well might talk about 80
Were they confided to a sieve-like ear.
And every day and hour of every year
Our little pal for Envy is a mark.
If with the patron at the games he'll park,
Or on the Campus both are playing ball, 85
"A very child of Fortune!" so say all.
Sometimes a creepy rumor trickling down
Out of the Rostra inundates the town,
And every one I meet inquires of me:
"Dear friend, you are so near the powers that be, 90
You stand with them so closely; you must know

Whatever may be so, or is not so.
What news about the Dacians? " " There is none
I heard of." " How you'll always have your fun! "
" May every god me damn, if anything   95
I know about it." " What's the news you bring
Of Caesar and the soldiers' promised land?
Is it Trinacria where he's going to hand
It out, or on our own Italian ground? "
And when I swear that nothing can be found   100
On me, they look upon me as a freak,
So deeply silent when I ought to speak.
In such, for wretched me the light of day
Is lost, but not without the prayers I say:
" When shall I gaze upon you, rustic bowers,   105
Now with old books or idle sleepy hours?
When shall I be allowed life's storm and stress
To drown in cups of blest forgetfulness?
O when before me shall be put the bean,
Pythagoras' kin, or well-anointed green   110
With bacon fat? O nights and feasts divine!
While friends and I before my hearth-god dine.
And when the Lar has got the part he craves,
I feed with what is left, my saucy slaves.
Then just as anybody cares to try,   115
Flagon or cup alike, the guest drinks dry.
And, subject to no crazy regulations,
One gets outside of mighty strong potations!
Another gets more pleasure, to his thinking,
By tippling at the wine with moderate drinking. 120
And conversation rises once again,
Not about house and grounds of other men,
Nor whether Lepos dances well or ill;

"Of the Mean and Sure Estate"

But conversation that more nearly will
Concern us all, where Ignorance is bad — 125
Whether mankind a greater blessing had
In riches than in virtue; what will draw
Together friends, interest or moral law;
What is the essence which we goodness call;
And what may be the highest good of all. 130
Meanwhile our neighbor Cervius will chatter
With old wives' tales for each and every matter.
If one of us the ills of wealth ignored
And praised Arellius and his careful hoard,
" Here's an old story," Cervius would begin. 135
" To a poor hole, a country mouse took in
A city mouse, old friends in days of yore.
The rugged, thrifty rustic spared his store
And yet he would relax a frugal mind
When he to hospitality inclined. 140
In short, he did not skimp the choice chick-peas
Nor the long oats; nor in his jaws with these
A raisin all dried up for many a day
Or scrap of bacon nibbled half away;
Desiring to cajole with varied fare 145
One who for simple diet did not care,
Fastidious, a very proud-toothed mouse.
The father and the master of the house
Stretched out upon a heap of this year's straw
Chewed spelt and darnel, pushing with his paw 150
Up to his guest the best of all the feast.
Then up and spake the little city beast:
' How can it help you, stubborn to abide
On this sheer slope, right in the woodland wide?
Why will you not the city and citizens 155

Prefer to the wild trees? Friend, let's go hence!
Believe me, on this earth both beast and man
With mortal souls live an allotted span.
And whether you be big or you be small
From Lethe you shall not escape at all.   160
Dear comrade, let's live merrily while we may.
Mind ye how brief is each wee creature's day.'
This utterance touched the field mouse to the soul;
Lightly he leapt out of his house and hole.
And both set out, each eager at the fall   165
Of night to creep under the city wall.
When midnight held the space of Heaven, each mouse
Set stealthy footprints in an affluent house,
Where ivory couches shone with scarlet cover;
From yesterday's great banquet was left over   170
Course upon course in baskets heaped up high.
On purple vestment stretched out royally
The field mouse by his host was duly placed;
And like a servant girt about the waist
The city mouse each course in order bore;   175
And like a servant licked each dish before
'Twas served. He on his couch in high estate
Rejoiced at the mutation of his fate
And played the role of guest mid Plenty's store;
Till sudden a loud noise smote at the door.   180
Each scuttled from his couch, pallid indeed,
And ran through that apartment at full speed
Shaking all over; while the mansion rung
Again as the Molossian hounds gave tongue.
The rustic spake: 'This life's no use to me!   185
Good night! me for my hole inside the tree,
All nice and safe, with scrubby bean and pea!' "

BOOK II

VII · MASTER AND SLAVE

TALK SEVEN is a dialogue between Horace and Davus his houseman. Davus does most of the talking, for it is his privilege to speak his mind fully at the Saturnalia, that Roman holiday in December when the slaves enjoyed a brief respite from their servitude. Davus is a stock figure from the comic stage; but Horace, as usual, changes the type into an individual, a voluble fellow who might be called, in our less formal discourse, "a smart aleck," whose language at times is shamelessly coarse, and who prefers the poster of a gladiator to a good picture — as some of our contemporaries are principally interested in the sporting columns of the newspaper.

While Davus expounds the Stoic lore which he has acquired from the doorkeeper of Crispinus, Horace listens with more or less patience. But the man riles his master whenever he gets personal, and finally when he twits Horace with his restless and moody melancholy, Horace explodes and breaks through the Saturnalian conventions with a threat. The scene is so well done that we almost forget it is a work of art.

In spite of his coarseness, Davus sometimes rises to his subject and, as Mulvaney would say, "occupies high ground." The verses beginning with " *Quisnam igitur liber?* — Who then is free? " are noble lines. When Davus learned them from Crispinus' janitor, he learned something good. We speak of a well-rounded character, an expression which comes from *teres atque rotundus*. I wonder how many times that familiar quotation has been used by notable English and American authors. The other day I ran across it in the *Antiquary* of Sir Walter Scott.

Talk Seven is one of the very latest. It may have been written in 31–30 B.C., shortly before the publication of the Second Book.

Talk Seven

Davus: I've waited quite a while; now it's my turn
To talk to you a little; but I'm durn
Afraid; I'm only a slave.
Horace: Ah! is it you,
Davus?
D.   Your servant, sir, and friendly, too,
And honest as a full-grown man can be.   5
H. The Saturnalia gave you liberty
To talk. Our forebears willed it. You can use
Your tongue and tell me anything you choose.
D. Some men are gladly constant to their vice;
Some wobble up and down. Now they'll be nice   10
To aim at what is right: at other times,
Addicted to all manner of vicious crimes.
Priscus was very conspicuous for his rings,
Wearing all three at once; but in all things
Fickle, he'd change his stripe with every hour.   15
Leaving his mansion and seignorial tower,
He'd plunge in a low dive, which none could be
Seen coming out of with impunity.
A whoremaster at Rome he would prefer
To live; in Athens, a philosopher.   20
Like all these weather gods, the man was born
For transformation, every night and morn.
And then there's Volanerius the clown,

Who, when arthritis did his fingers down,
Hired a man, and paid him by the day,   25
To pick up all the dice he cast in play,
And put them back into the box again.
Yet to his vice he constant would remain —
More of a man and better altogether
Than one who tugs, then slackens at the tether. —   30
H. Born to be hanged! All day you think you've got
To talk? What is the point of all this rot?
D. I'm telling you. It's you, as you might say.
H. The point! The point! You scalawag!
D.   Every day
You sound the praises of the men of old.   35
Their manners and their fortunes; and behold,
If God should put you back into their use
And wont, it's more than quickly you'd refuse,
Either because, for all your solemn clack,
You think it's far from better to go back,   40
Or else you are disloyal to what's good,
And will not pull your feet out of the mud.
When you're in Rome, you want the country! When
You turn into a hayseed, Oh! 'tis then
You praise the city, all the stars above.   45
If nobody asks you out to dine, you love
Your simple salad; nobody could hope
To drag you out to dinner with a rope.
How free and easy! Really, now you think
You're lucky when you haven't got to drink.   50
But if Maecenas calls you out to sup
Late at his table when it's all lit up,
" Oil for my lamps this instant! What's the matter?
Nobody here? " You bustle and you blatter

And raise the roof; and fast away you fly.   55
If Mulvius and your parasites come by,
Eager to get a little bit to eat,
They curse you in a way I won't repeat
When they go off. "I may be a light weight,"
Says he, "My stomach drives me to a date.   60
When I smell food, my nose goes curlicue;
I'm shiftless; and I like a drink or two.
But you are lower down than I can reach —
You cover up your vice with pompous speech."
I cost you fifty bucks paid down by you —   65
But how am I the sillier of the two?
Now please don't give a dirty look like that!
Hold off your hands and temper while I chat
With you, exactly telling you what for.
I learned it from Cuspinus' janitor.   70
Another's wife gathers you in for loot;
Davus is captured by a prostitute.
You for a married wench; I for a whore;
Which of us two deserves the cross the more?
When in the blood the cries of Nature range   75
I make a cash down payment of small change,
And naked in the light, the girl avails
To take the strokes of many turgid tails;
Or with lascivious buttocks gives a course
For riding bareback on the Trojan horse.   80
But when she says good night, I shall not be
Afraid of any notoriety,
Nor yet of anyone who takes my place
Holding me up to insult and disgrace,
One better off or comelier to be seen,   · 85
Who'll sprinkle up the place where I have been.

But you, all grand insignia cast aside,
Your Roman toga and your civic pride,
When under a hood, your hair oil you conceal,
Why are you not yourself what you reveal? 90
No more the title of a judge you fancy,
But steal down half-lit lanes, just like a pansy.
A door may let you in, but you're on fire
With fear, that burns more hotly than desire.
Well, what's the difference, whether you get whipped, 95
Gelt with a knife, or in a cupboard slipped
To hide your baseness, by a knowing jade,
While close against your knees, your head you've laid?
As for the husband of the erring dame,
You're in his power, both of you the same; 100
Under his thumb you rightly both shall be,
You the seducer, even more than she
Who need not change her place nor change her dress.
She fears her lover and distrusts him. Less
Her fault than yours, who go beneath the yoke. 105
Thus by an irate master, you'll be broke,
And render up your holdings and, to boot,
Your life, your body, and your good repute.
Perhaps you will escape, and one could swear
Your future fears would teach you to beware. 110
But, given the opportunity again,
From Terror and from Death you'll not refrain.
O total slave! What beast that ever gets
Free once, would crave to go back to the nets?
You don't commit adultery, you say. 115
Just so I ain't a thief in any way.
Your silver plate, I prudently pass by;

Master and Slave

But, take away the danger that comes nigh,
Off like a shot, unbridled nature strains
Forward the moment you remove the reins. 120
Are you the master, whom the rule of things
And men so far beneath my slavery brings
That Praetor's rod with three or fourfold hit
From abject terror cannot manumit?
And now another truth, I'd like to state, 125
Added to all the rest, of no less weight.
Is one who serves a slave an underslave?
(The likes of you that sort of title gave)
Or am I only a fellow-slave with you?
I ask you for the name that rings most true. 130
Say, what am I? What name do I deserve
When you another miserably serve,
Responsive to his wish in every thing,
Just like a jumping jack upon a string?
Who then is free? Himself who rules with brains, 135
Fearless of poverty, or death, or chains:
Who quells desire, spurns honors to the ground,
Whose strength is in himself, all smooth and round,
So nothing on that surface from outside
Can stick, but from the polish it will slide 140
Away. Misfortune's blows no harm shall bring;
Her shock is beaten back with broken wing.
But anything like this, you'll never know
For yours. Out of your wad five grand will go
For a light girl, who'll show you to the door, 145
And down upon your head cold water pour,
And call you back again. You're at her beck
And call. That monstrous yoke shake off your neck.
Go say: " I'm free. I'm free." Ah no, not much!

No lenient master rides your mind. With touch 150
Of spur, he pricks you deep when you stand still;
Driving you onward all against your will,
All sick and weary of the goad and rein.
Over a fresco you have grown insane;
At Pausias, his picture, you have got 155
To gawk and gape like a poor idiot.
Is idle folly less for you than me,
When Fulvius or Rutuba I see
Or Pacideianus, strong of limb and tall,
Daubed in red paint or charcoal on a wall? 160
They seem to be alive; they thrust and parry,
With weapons that look real; but when I tarry,
Poor Davus loafs. Your attitude bespeaks
A connoisseur of genuine antiques.
If I am tempted by a steaming pie, 165
There's nothing much too bad for such as I.
Do you, magnanimous in mind and soul,
Avoid rich banquets or the flowing bowl?
Why worse for me than you the stomach's call?
I buy a feast with whippings; are you all 170
Exempt, when you are vanquished by your vice,
Craving for dainties bought at no small price?
The viands without end that you seek out
Turn bitter in the belly; and the gout
Cripples your feet. Deluded they refuse 175
To bear above the ground, as was their use,
Your body given o'er to aches and pains.
Why is the slave more guilty, when he gains
A bunch of grapes, to make an evening meal,
Traded for some bronze strigil, he might steal? 180
The man who for his paunch sells an estate,

Master and Slave

Of equal value with a slave must rate.
Moreover, there is not one single hour
You can be with yourself; you have no power
Long days of leisure rightly to employ;
Your solitude you never can enjoy;
Shunning yourself, you wander here and there,
Trying with wine or sleep to banish Care.
In vain: for that black comrade still draws nigh
To follow wheresoever you would fly.
H.   A rock!
D.   What for?
H.   Bring javelins for me!
D. The man is mad — or making poetry!
H. If you don't get out quick and stay out, too,
Ninth farmhand on my Sabine Farm for you!

BOOK II

VIII · THE BANQUET

THIS Talk is a δεῖπνον or *cena*. The δεῖπνον was served in Greek from Plato to Athenaeus; and the *cena* in Latin from Lucilius to Macrobius. Some were solemn, others not. This one could hardly be called a feast of reason and a flow of soul. It was far less dignified than the host intended. Poor old Nasidienus is one of the funny figures of fiction. Fundanius' account of the bill of fare is intentionally funny, for Fundanius was a comic poet and knew a laugh when he heard it.

In his third Satire, Boileau has made a *rechauffé* of this *cena*, and the author of "L'Art Poétique" has elsewhere shown his allegiance to his master. For his seventh Satire, he lifts one passage from the "Sermon against Adultery" and another from the talk with Trebatius. For his Eighth, he cribs the contrast between the merchant and the ant. In the Ninth he plays a variation on the gossip about Petillius Capitolinus. One might continue *ad nauseam*, for Boileau oozes Horace at every pore. But he is only one of many who have imbibed inspiration from the wise and witty friend of Maecenas, of Virgil, and of ancient and modern civilization.

Talk Eight

HORACE: How did you like it, as a dinner guest
Of Nasidienus, with much money blest?
When I asked after you, to dine with me
They told me yesterday that you must be
Drinking with him since twelve.
FUNDANIUS: Ah! that was prime! 5
I never in my life had such a time.
H. Well, if it does not get upon your nerves,
Please give me what you had for the *hors-d'œuvres*,
An angry belly to propitiate.
F. First a Lucanian boar, served on a plate,   10
And captured when the south wind blew the least
Harshly, so said the father of the feast;
With turnips, lettuces and radishes,
And round about were other relishes,
Hot to the taste and with an acrid bite   15
A lassitudinous stomach to excite.
The pungent water-parsnip, pickled fish,
And dregs of Coan wine garnished the dish.
When these were taken away, a well-girt knave
Rubbed down the maple table with a brave   20
Wool serviette dyed in purple; and another
Swept up the leavings which the guests might bother.
Then like an Attic virgin straight and tall,
Who carries corn to Ceres' festival,
Swarthy Hydaspes marches with the wine   25
Of Caecuba, and Chian without brine

The Banquet

Is poured by Alcon. Then the profiteer,
" Maecenas, Alban or Falernian's here,
If they be more delectable," he quoth,
" You can have either, for we have them both."   30
H. Poor Croesus! But, Fundanius, tell me who
Around his table made the sport for you?
I'm dying to know.
F.   Top of the heap, was I,
And next to me Viscus of Thurii.
As I remember, Varius was below;   35
Vibidius and Balatro — " shadows " so-
Called of Maecenas, which a man of station
Could take along without an invitation.
And either proved a very lively ghost.
Then Nomentanus, just above the host,   40
And Porcius on the underside, who makes
Himself ridiculous, gobbling cheesy cakes.
For Nomentanus, if there lurked a doubt
About a dish, his finger pointed out
Just what it was. The rest of us, I say,   45
Through fish and fowl and oysters worked our way,
Different in taste from any we had known,
And this was proven in no uncertain tone.
Turbot livers and plaice he handed o'er
To me. I never tasted them before.   50
He told me too how honey-apples soon
Grew ruddier, picked beneath a waning moon.
What difference that could make, might be made clear
If he could tell it to a listening ear.
Vibidius to Balatro then: " I'm thinking,   55
Unless we do some pretty ruinous drinking,
We'll all die unavenged." He needs must seek

For mammoth goblets. Pallid grew the cheek
Of the entertainer; for he could not bear
Hard drinkers who will freely curse and swear,   60
And anyhow because a palate fine
Is vitiated with a fiery wine.
Balatro and Vibidius poured, in right
Great Allifan tumblers, all the wine in sight;
We followed their example, one by one,   65
Save at the bottom table there was none
To harm the flagons, or the host to slight,
For each picked guest was there a parasite.
Stretched on a dish, with many a floating prawn,
An eel was served, who was about to spawn.   70
" Better will be the flesh," the master said,
" If netted just before the eggs are laid;
But if she's captured after parturition
She'll be in very inferior condition.
The sauce is mixed this way: Take olive oil   75
First from the press, grown on Venafran soil;
Wine five years old, born this side of the sea,
Pour on while simmering; Coan wine will be
Better than any, when the sauce is cooked.
White pepper is not to be overlooked,   80
Nor vinegar, as you perhaps discern,
From Methymnean grape juice on the turn;
Colewort and bitter horse-heal, first have I
Shown as ingredients for this cookery;
Unwashed sea-urchins would Curtillus use,   85
Such shellfish better flavor interfuse
Than seafood pickled in a salt sea wash."
Just then the heavy awning came kersmash
Down on the platter, dragging in its wake

The Banquet

Such grimy dust as stormwinds never make 90
When booming over the Campanian flat.
We feared that something more might come of that;
After we sensed the danger was no more
We rose to the occasion as before.
But Rufus hung his head and sobbed and cried 95
As though a son before his time had died;
And no one knows what would have been the end
If cheerful Nomentanus, his good friend,
Had not philosophized: " Ah, Fortune, now
Which of the gods more cruel is than Thou? 100
Still making game of all the human race? "
Varius, with his napkin to his face,
Tried to choke down the laughter that arose.
Balatro, always turning up his nose:
" Life is like that," said he, " and there you are; 105
Your name and fame will never be at par
With what you try to do. They will not be
Responsive. Here I'm treated lavishly
And you tormented sorely with anxiety.
Your bread is burnt; your sauce is mixed all wrong; 110
Some of the slaves are girt too short or long;
They are not picked to wait on table well.
Accidents happen; as your awning fell
Just now. Your stable boy may trip and fall
And break your dish. You're like a general 115
When you are entertaining at a dinner;
Bad luck will only stimulate a winner;
Good luck your talents only serves to hide."
Said Nasidienus: " May the gods provide
A blessing all your kindness to requite. 120
This guest is a good man and most polite."

He called then for his slippers suddenly
And left us. On the couches you can see
Each guest is whispering in his neighbor's ear,
Small, soft secretive sounds you scarcely hear.   125
H. There never was a play I'd sooner see.
What else was a great laugh? Enlighten me.
F. Well, while Vibidius asked the waiters whether
All the big cups were broken altogether,
For when he called for wine it would not come   130
And all of our remarks, however dumb,
We took as jokes and roared at every one,
And meanwhile Balatro helped us making fun —
Lo and behold, Nasidienus, thou
Returned among us, with an altered brow,   135
By dint of art thy fortune to renew.
The slaves that followed in thy retinue
Upon a monstrous platter bore amain,
The fragmentary members of a crane
Decked with much salt and not without fine meal;   140
A white goose fed on figs must here reveal
Its liver; and the shoulders of the hare,
Much better to the taste if eaten spare,
Without the loins; and also here we find
Rooks with burnt breast, and doves without behind;   145
The food was good enough, but not so good
To listen to his talk about the food;
Nature and cause alike the master told,
And each and every detail would unfold.
We in retaliation ran away,   150
And tasted nothing more he served that day.
As if Canidia's breath each dainty makes
More venomous than Africa, its snakes.

THE LIBRARY
ST. MARY'S COLLEGE OF MARYLAND
ST. MARY'S CITY, MARYLAND 20686

70115